Circular Coas Cornwa

by Chris Adams

Published in 1997 by

The Moor, Dale and Mountain Press.
South Down.
Bratton Fleming.
Devon. U.K.
EX31 4TQ.

ISBN 1 899183 35 3

© Copyright Christopher Adams 1997

No part of this publication may be reproduced in full or in part. in any form. without the written permission of the publisher.

The Moor, Dale and Mountain Press,
Bratton Fleming

IMPORTANT NOTE. Whilst every effort has been made by the author to determine the most appropriate and correct routes whilst actually walking the paths no responsibility whatsoever can be accepted by the author or the publisher for precision at time of use by the purchaser or by anyone.
Anyone using any part of the routes described in this publication does so entirely at their own discretion.
Occasionally a path that is frequently used by the public and that is not necessarily a public right of way has been included within this series.
All stated distances are approximations.
All of the heights above sea level and grid references stated in this publication are approximate and are derived from the O. S. Landranger maps for the area which are Landranger 190. 200. 201. 203 and 204.

How to use the guide

Sennen Cove, Land's End and Mill Bay.

On the A30 turn right about 3km (2 miles) before Land's End on to a minor road to Sennen Cove. At Sennen Cove continue to the car park at 1 which is at the end of the road, near the lifeboat station.

This part of the page shows how the walk can be found on a road map or from road signs.

All the sketch maps share the same approximate scale which is 2cm per kilometre or 3.2cm per mile and approximate grid north is towards the top of the page.

There should be sufficient space on the sketch maps to mark any locations of your own.

The heavy line on the sketch maps is the approximate mean sea level and not the edge of the cliff.

All the walks are circular walks and can be started at any point. The figures before the brackets at the start of paragraphs are the locations on the sketch.

Grid references are shown in brackets for walkers who like to use maps.

If it is probable that the walk is impassable in winter a note is included in the text of any available alternatives. When referring to rivers and riverbanks the text sometimes refers to "downstream near the left bank" which does mean the left side of the river when looking downstream and "upstream near the left bank" which does mean the left side of the river when looking upstream.

1.(349263) From the car park our route follows the Coast Path south for about 3km to go through the Land's End complex and the adjacent small animal farm to 2, at the far side of Mill Bay.

2.(357238) At the far side of Mill Bay a house can be seen on the other side of a valley through which a small brook flows. Our route leaves the Coast Path to follow the signed footpath that follows a fairly well worn path up the near side of the valley and along the top of the near side of the valley, to go through a gate and into a field. Our route goes directly across the field to a pair of gates in the corner where it goes over the stile by the left gate and around the right side of the field to continue through a gateway and

8km (5 miles).
The scenery is very good.
Usually good walking all year round.
Overall from about sea level up to 101 metres.
Some modest slopes and a steep one.
There is a car park at 1.
There are tearooms and a pub at Sennen Cove.

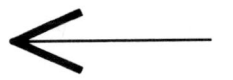

This part of the page provides an overview of the walk and the facilities.

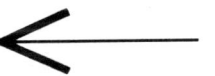

diagonally across the next field to the furthest corner. Here our route goes over the stile next to the gate and on to a track that goes around the right hand side of Trevilley and at the first T-junction goes straight across into a farmyard at 3.

3.(358245) Our route goes straight across the farmyard, over some concrete steps, around the right hand side of a field, over a stone stile and across the left side of a field to go through a small gate, over another stone stile and in front of the cottages to the road at 4.

The text thoroughly describes the route and each walk has been selected to include the most contrasting range of natural scenery.

4.(356248) Our route turns left on the road and then goes straight across at the T-junction to go down the drive to Treeve Moor House. As the drive bears left our route leaves the drive to continue on and then right to go over some stones, or an ancient stone stile, and into a field. Our route goes directly up the field to go through a small gate near the top left corner and into another field. Continuing across the top of this field our route then goes over a stone stile in the corner and on towards the houses to go over another stile on the coast side of them. Our route goes across the top of the field until the wall on the right ends and here our route goes through a small gate on to a lane at 5.

5.(352259) Our route continues in the same direction along the lane to follow it around to the right and on for about a further 300m to take the footpath down on the left which is before the last bungalow. At the end of the footpath our route turns left on the road to return to the car park at 1.

Over moors, heaths and mountains it is frequently useful at some times of the year to carry a compass and on the walks to which this applies approximate compass directions are included. All distances stated are approximate.

The word "lane" is used to describe a road on which two vehicles could not usually pass and the word "track" is used when the condition of the surface makes it unlikely to be used by most cars.

Cornwall

The numbers indicate the approximate location of the start of the walks on the corresponding page number.

Circular Coast Walks Cornwall

From the north coast boundary with Devon to Plymouth Sound.

Marsland Mouth, Duckpool and Morwenstow	page 1
Northcott Mouth, Coombe and Duckpool	page 3
Bude, Widemouth Sands and Helebridge	page 4
Millook, Dizzard and Trebarfoote Coombe	page 5
Crackington Haven and St. Gennys	page 7
Crackington Haven, Cambeak and Pengold	page 8
Boscastle, Newmills, Beeny and Pentargon	page 9
Boscastle and Rocky Valley	page 10
Tintagel, Trebarwith Strand and Rocky Valley	page 12
Trebarwith Strand, Dannonchapel Valley and Treligga	page 14
Porthquin and Port Isaac	page 16
Pentireglaze, Pentire Point and New Polzeath	page 17
Padstow, Stepper Point and Trevone	page 18
St. Agnes Head, Porthtowan and St. Agnes Beacon	page 20
Portreath, Coombe and Tehidy Country Park	page 22
Hell's Mouth and Coombe	page 23
St. Ives, River Cove, Wicca and Trevalgan	page 24
Zennor, Wicca, Zennor Head and Poniou	page 26
Woon Gumpus Common, Pendeen Watch and Bosullow Common	page 28
Sennen Cove and Maen Dower	page 30
Sennen Cove, Land's End and Mill Bay	page 31
Porthcurno, Penberth Cove, Nanjizal and Gwennap Head	page 32
Lamorna Cove and St. Loy's Cove	page 34
Perranuthnoe and Cudden Point	page 35
Mullion Cove, Predannack Head and Ogo-dour Cove	page 36
Predannack Wollas, Vellan Head and Kynance Cove	page 37
The Lizard, Kynance Cove and Lizard Point	page 38
The Lizard, Bass Point and Gwavas	page 39
Porthallow, Nare Point and Gillan	page 40
Manaccan, Dennis Head and Helford	page 41
Percuil River, Zone Point and Porthmellin Head	page 43
Penare, Hemmick Beach, Dodman Point and Gorran Haven	page 44
Fowey, Polkerris and Gribbin Head	page 45
Pencarrow, Pont Pill and Polruan	page 46
Cawsand, Rame Head and Penlee Point	page 47
Cremyll, Empacombe and Kingsand	page 48

Before starting a walk please check page 21 for any additional information.

Marsland Mouth, Duckpool and Morwenstow.

On the A39, Bude to Bideford, turn left about 5km (3 miles) north of Kilkhampton on to a minor road signed to Shop and Morwenstow. There is a car park at Morwenstow, at 1, which is at the end of the road, between the church and the tearoom.

17km (10 miles) or two walks of 7km (4 miles) and 11km (7 miles).
The scenery is outstanding. Not only is the cliff area outstanding but the inland part is very varied.
Usually good walking all year round.
Some steep slopes.
Overall from 10m up to 144m.
There are car parks at Morwenstow and Duckpool.
There is a tearoom and a pub at Morwenstow.

1.(206152) At Morwenstow our route enters the churchyard by the lych gate and turns right, turning right again at the bottom of that path and then left over a stone stile. From here our route is along the side of a barn and continues down to the footbridge and then directly up through the gate at the top of the field to turn right at the next gate to pass between the farm buildings at Westcott Farm at 2.

2.(207157) From Westcott Farm our route follows the track north. After about 100m the track veers to the right but our route continues directly on, keeping to the right of the hedge, to a stile at 3.

3.(208160) Over the stile our route follows a track to the right and then a lane to the left to Cornackey Farm where our path turns right, through the farm yard, to a track into a field. Four or five fields in front of that spot Marsland Manor can be seen. Our route continues along the top of the field keeping near to the hedge on the right to the next field gate. From there our route goes diagonally down across the field to a stone stile near the corner then across the next field towards Marsland Manor to another stile. From there our route goes down into a combe, across a footbridge and up the other side following the track up and to the right to Marsland Manor at 4.

4.(217168) At Marsland Manor there is a

Page 1

choice of paths. Either straight on through the buildings and then right on to the lane or right before the buildings and over a stile on to the lane where our route turns left for just over a hundred metres and then turns left down the first disused lane. After a few hundred metres there is a cottage on the right and here our route turns off to the left to the Coast Path at 5.

5.(212174) At Marsland Mouth our route turns left on the Coast Path which is fairly obvious south to Duckpool at 8. About 2km south of Marsland Mouth there is a path down the cliff for a few metres to a hut. at 7. once used by a vicar of Morwenstow when he felt like writing poetry.

8.(201117) At Duckpool where the Coast Path meets a tarmac lane our route turns inland to a junction then turns left and then immediately right down another lane. Over the footbridge and past the last cottage on the left at Combe our route follows the lane around to the left at 9(210118) and then after a further 150m leaves the lane to follow a path off to the left. Keeping the stream to the left for just over 1km our route then goes over a footbridge on the left and then continues up the bank for about 15m before turning right up to a junction. Turning left at that junction our route goes up to. and through. a gate on the right and then continues to a lane on which our route turns left down into Woodford at 10.

10.(219135) In Woodford our route turns left on the road and. before the telephone kiosk, turns left along a footpath into a field where our route turns to the right. keeping to the right of the hedge, to a stile from where, almost directly across two fields can be seen Eastway Manor. Our route heads towards the right side of Eastway Manor going over two stiles in the intervening hedge on the way. At Eastway Manor our route runs between a wall and a hedge to a lane. Our route goes across the lane into a field and then turns right into, and directly across, the adjacent field to a stone stile. From the stile our route goes across the field keeping a few degrees to the right to a path around Stanbury Farm at 11.

11.(210140) At the end of this path our route goes directly across a lane and on to a track to turn right over a stone stile at the far end of the low barn. Directly across that field is a stile from which can be seen a farmstead called Tonacombe. Our route heads for the nearest corner of Tonacombe Farm, to a gate and then goes more or less straight on along a track to a field. Directly in front of that spot, a few fields away, is the pub at Morwenstow. Our route goes across that field keeping close to the hedge on the right to cross a stile about half way across the field. Our route goes across the small stream in the combe and then bears slightly to the right. ignoring the path to the left and then goes directly across a field to a stile near the pub. out on to the lane and then left, down to the car park.

SHORT ROUTES.

Marsland Mouth Part. 7km. This route follows the notes to Marsland Mouth and then follows the Coast Path to the second combe with a stream and then takes the next path inland from 6(200152) to Morwenstow Church.

Duckpool Part. 11km. Starting at Morwenstow and following the track that goes towards the coast from between the churchyard and the tearoom this route keeps to the left side of the valley to the Coast Path where it turns left and then the main notes can be followed.

Page 2

Northcott Mouth, Coombe and Duckpool.

On the A39, Bude to Bideford, turn left about 1km after Stratton on to a minor road signed to Poughill and continue on a minor road to Northcott Mouth.

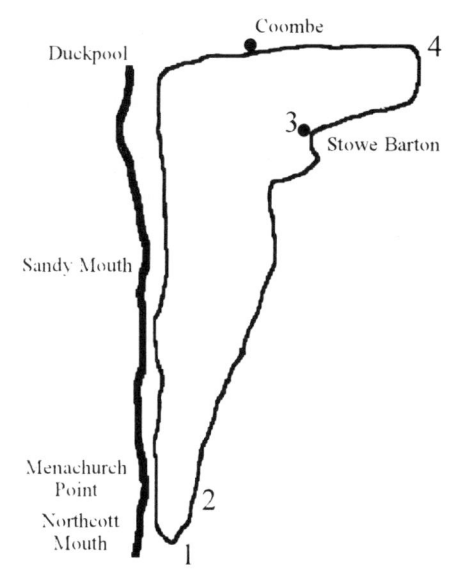

10km (6 miles).
The scenery is very good. The inland section offers some very good views and then follows woodland paths.
Can be muddy between Northcott Mouth and Stowe Barton after rain in winter.
One steep slope.
Overall from about sea level up to 128m.
There is a car park at Northcott Mouth.
There is a tearoom at Northcott Mouth and there are tearooms and pubs in Bude.

1.(203085) From Northcott Mouth our path goes inland and north east past some cottages to 2 where the track turns abruptly right to Dunsmouth Farm.

2.(204090) Here our route leaves the track and continues directly on, keeping to the right of the field and then joining a track to a lane. Our route goes directly over the lane and into the field in which it keeps to the right. In the next field our route turns right through a gate on to a track with banked hedges to a lane where our route turns left down to Stowe Barton, the first farm on the right, near 3.

3.(211112) About 100m before the farm our route goes through a gate in the wall on the right and curves across the field on to a track which ends at a bungalow. Here our route goes through the field gate on the right and down the middle of the field to join a track to a stile. Over the stile our route continues down through the woods to turn right on a track over a bridge and then immediately left to go over the next bridge at 4.

4.(220116) After going over this bridge our route turns left on a track for about 1km to join a lane at Coombe. Continuing directly along that lane our route then turns left at the junction and then immediately right down to the Coast Path which is on the left and fairly obvious back to Northcott Mouth.

Bude, Widemouth Sands and Helebridge.

From the A39 take the A3072 into Bude. This walk starts from the large car park on the left, in Bude, adjacent to the Tourist Information Centre at 1.

9km (6 miles).
The scenery is good. The inland part is over typical farmland and along the side of the Bude canal.
Can be slightly muddy in winter over arable farmland between Widemouth Bay and Helebridge.
A couple of very gentle slopes.
Overall from about sea level up to 60m.
There is a car park in Bude at 1.
There are tearooms and pubs in Bude.

1.(210059) From the car park our route turns left on the road to cross the bridge and then immediately right to be on the south bank of the canal from where the Coast Path is well signed as it goes out to the cliff. About 3.5km from Bude the Coast Path has to come inland of a house with a garden that goes to the edge of the cliff and here our route leaves the Coast Path.

2.(200030) Our route turns left to cross the coast road and enters a field at a stile. From the stile our route goes away from the road and across the field to the top left corner to go over another stile and in the next field our route veers slightly to the left, aiming for a point midway between the hedge on the right and the brow of the hill on the left, to go over another stile. Across the top of this field our route comes to another stile and from there our route continues down across the field, keeping slightly to the left, towards the houses in the valley, to a gate that can be seen from the stile. Through this gate our route curves down and to the left on a track to a lane. On this lane our route turns right towards the road near Helebridge at 3.

3.(215038) Our route turns left either on the permissive path just before the brook or on the road for the few metres to the path that turns left along the nearest side of the canal. Keeping on the left bank of the canal for about 1km, to just past the cottages on the left, our route then goes over the canal on a tarmac bridge and continues down the other side to Bude.

Millook, Dizzard and Trebarfoote Coombe.

From the A39, Bude to Wadebridge, turn right about 4km (3 miles) south of Bude on to a minor road signed Widemouth Bay. At Widemouth Bay turn left on to the coast road for about 2km through Wanson, to a cliff top car park on the right, at 1, at Penhalt Cliff.

8km (5 miles).
The scenery is outstanding. Most of the inland section is through a wooded valley with a stream.
Usually good walking all year.
Some steep slopes.
Overall from about sea level up to 164m.
There is a car park at 1.
There are tearooms and pubs at Crackington Haven and Widemouth Bay.

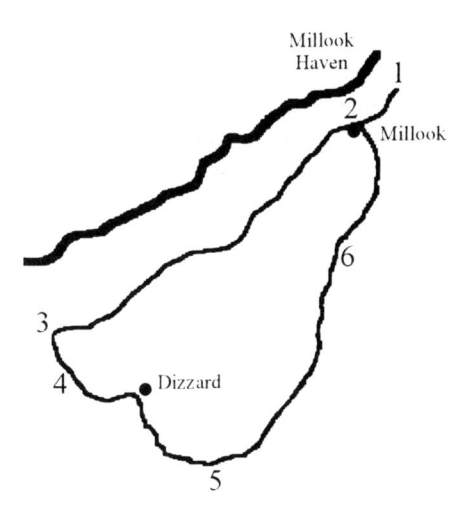

1.(188004) Our route follows the Coast Path south to Millook Haven at 2(185000) and then continues on the Coast Path for just over 2km to where our route turns off at 3.

3.(162989) *It is possible to miss where our route turns left off the Coast Path. There is a very deep and steep sided combe that has a lot of gorse on the near side on the Coast Path about 500m past this junction.* This junction is where the Coast Path is going through some low oaks and scrub and curves to the right as it dips slightly. As the Coast Path curves back to the left there are some steps leading up on the left through the scrub. Here our route leaves the Coast Path and goes up these steps and through the scrub on a path that curves to the left to a stile. Our route goes over the stile, keeps to the left for a few metres and then goes up the field keeping to the left side of the wet area of scrub on the right. At the top of the field our route goes over a stile and across the track to then go immediately over another stile by the side of a field gate. Our route then turns left in the field to continue along the right hand side of the field bank and then down into the wood. Keeping to the left in the wood our route follows a fairly obvious path that curves down and to the right as far as a footbridge on the left at 4.

4.(164985) In summer this footbridge can be obscured by vegetation. Our route goes over the footbridge and continues up the left side of the field on the other side of the valley to a stile. Over this stile our route goes up the left side of the field to a field gate at the end of a track. Turning left through this gate our route goes along the track to Dizzard Farm and turns right on the lane at the end of the track. Just under 500m along the lane there is a track on the left at 5.

5.(169980) Our route follows the track past the farm at Trengayor and to the left of the house to just past where the track widens noticeably and there is a field gate on the left. Here our route goes through the field gate and down a narrow track between two hedge banks and on down through the wood. Crossing the brook on some stepping stones our route continues downstream along a path that for most of the way is near the left bank of the stream, to a fork. Here our route takes the right fork to cross over the footbridge and to continue across the field in front of the house and on to a track. On the track our route turns left, past the house, and over some steps into the first field on the left. Over these steps our route continues to the right, almost down the centre of the field, to the far end where another set of steps, near the corner, takes our route into the wood. Bearing right our route continues downstream near the right bank of the brook to where there is a footbridge just before a thatched cottage at 6.

6.(181998) Over the footbridge our route continues down the track, now with the cottage on the right, and on for about 800m to a lane at Millook where our route turns right on the lane, or follows the Coast Path, back to the car park at 1.

Around Millook and Crackington there are some steep cliffs and exciting views with interesting folded cliff formations around Crackington which gave its name to the local geological series.

South of Crackington the more usual image of the Cornwall coast presents itself with moderate cliffs and small fishing villages where the coves are sufficiently large to offer shelter to the small boats, as at Boscastle. South of Boscastle the mining area of Cornwall also begins.

However, around Crackington the coastal hills are sufficiently high to offer shelter to the valleys just inland and here spring arrives very early and the mildness of late summer tends to linger.

Crackington Haven and St. Gennys.

From the A39, Bude to Wadebridge, turn right about 11km (7 miles) south of Bude on to a minor road signed to Crackington Haven. The car park at 1 is adjacent to the pub near the shore at Crackington Haven.

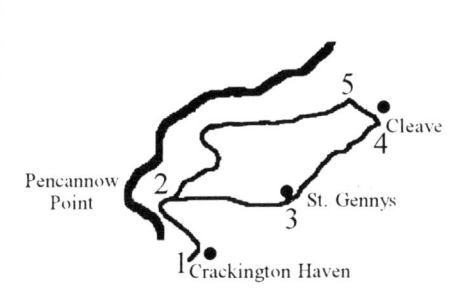

5km (3 miles).
The scenery is outstanding.
The inland section can be muddy after heavy rain in winter.
Some steep slopes.
Overall from about sea level up to 131m.
There is a car park at 1.
There are tearooms and a pub at Crackington Haven.

1.(143968) Our route goes through the car park and at the rear of the car park the Coast Path turns left on to the lane and then turns right for a few metres to a footpath on the left. Here our route follows the Coast Path up between two cottages and continues up the hillside to the hill that overlooks the bay and then goes over a stile into a field to continue near the cliff top to another stile at 2.

2.(142971) Here our route leaves the Coast Path to enter a field and continues along the right side of the fence to a gate. Over the stile next to the gate our route continues in the same direction, near the side of the bank on the left, past St. Gennys Church on the left, to the corner of the field where there is a stile. Over the stile our path follows a track down to the lane at 3.

3.(150971) On the lane our route turns left for about 30m to take the first lane down to the right. When the lane forks our route keeps to the left to go down the gravel track to the left, towards St. Gennys House. At the next fork our route keeps to the left of the tree and continues past the house to a stile. Over this stile our route heads across the field approximately towards a point midway between the high cliff ahead and the farm some way over to the right. At the far side of the field our route follows a path down to the right, through a wood, to a footbridge at 4.

4.(153975) Over the footbridge our route follows a track up to the right and over a stile. Our route continues up the right hand side of the field to the gate at the top right corner and turns left along the hedge side to follow a path to the Coast Path at 5(153978) where our route turns left back to Crackington Haven.

Crackington Haven, Cambeak and Pengold.

From the A39, Bude to Wadebridge, turn right about 11km (7 miles) south of Bude on to a minor road signed to Crackington Haven. The car park at 1 is adjacent to the pub near the shore at Crackington Haven.

6km (4 miles).
The scenery is outstanding. Much of the inland part is through a wooded valley.
The inland section can be muddy in winter.
Some modest and one steep slope.
Overall from about sea level up to 170m.
There is a car park at 1.
There are tearooms and a pub at Crackington Haven.

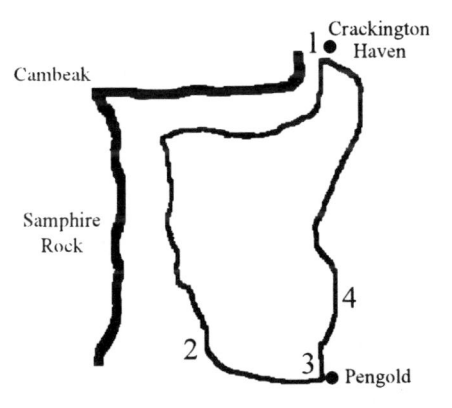

1.(143968) The Coast Path is fairly obvious west for about 1km to Cambeak and then south for just over 1.5km to where our route leaves the Coast Path at 2.
2.(132948) The Coast Path dips slightly through an area of scrub with a bare rock face about 6m high on the left and then goes up a few steps from the top of which it is possible to look back along the cliffs and through a sea arch. Here our route leaves the Coast Path and turns left through a small area of gorse and then continues up the field, keeping slightly to the right, to a stile in the corner. Our route goes over the stile and turns left on the lane for about 20m to then go over a stile on the right and into a field. Our route goes down the field, keeping slightly to the right, to cross over a footbridge at the bottom and then continues up the next field, keeping slightly to the left, to the top of the field not far from the buildings at Pengold at 3.
3.(138945) At Pengold our route continues to the left from the farm buildings, northwards, across the top of the field with the valley down to the right. Almost directly across that field is a pair of gates and our route continues through the left gate and then immediately through a gate on the right to continue along the top of the field with the valley down to the right and then over a stile in the first corner. From this stile our route continues on down with a hedge bank on the right hand side and when that hedge bank turns abruptly away to the right our route continues directly down the field to join a track that veers to the right and down through the trees for about 20m to 4.
4.(140951) Here our route fords the brook on the left. Over the stile on the other side of the brook our route crosses the rough grass for about 50m to where four paths meet near the stream. Our route continues downstream near to the left bank for about 1km and then goes across the stream on a footbridge to continue downstream on some broad paths and then along a lane to a junction where our route turns left back to the car park at 1.

Boscastle, Newmills, Beeny and Pentargon.

Entering Boscastle on the B3263 from the north east there is a car park on the left near the visitor centre at 1.

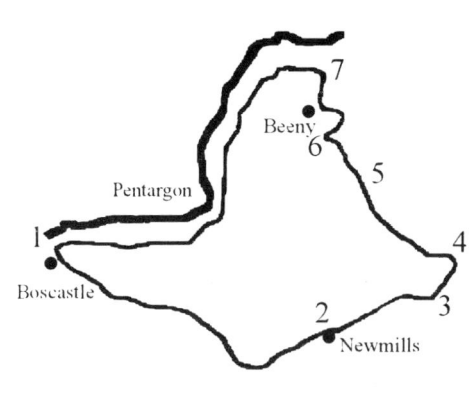

8km (5 miles).
The scenery is outstanding. The inland part includes the valley of the River Valency and some varied countryside.
Good walking all year with a few muddy places. After exceptionally heavy storms in winter it might not be possible to go up the river valley in flood conditions.
Overall from 15m up to 160 metres.
Some modest slopes.
There is a car park at 1.
There are tearooms and pubs in Boscastle.

1.(098914) From the car park our route follows the footpath upstream near the left bank of the River Valency for about 2km. to a hamlet called Newmills at 2.

2.(115911) At Newmills our route crosses a track and then follows a path up to the left that is signed "St. Juliot Church." Just over 500m along this path there is a ruined cottage on the right and then our route enters a field. Continuing along the top of the field our route goes past a house and garden on the left to a few metres before the far corner where there is a field gate on the left at 3.

3.(124914) At this field gate our route turns left. up the side of the adjacent field. to a track near a corner of the wood. Our route continues along this track. with the wood to the left. to a field gate on the left. at 4. about 25m before a tarmac lane.

4.(125915) Our route goes through this field gate and continues close to the field hedge on the right to go through a gap in the corner and across the next field. keeping slightly to the right to a stile in the hedge bank on the opposite side of the field. Over this stile our route continues in approximately the same direction to a stile in the hedge bank on the opposite side of the field. Over this stile our route keeps slightly to the left across the field to a stile in the hedge bank and over this stile keeps slightly to the left to go over a stile and on to a road at 5.

5.(120920) Our route goes across the road and down the track to Trebyla Farm and when the track bends sharp right our route goes over the second stile on the left into the small field adjacent to the farm and continues diagonally across the field to a stile in the far right corner. Over this stile our route goes almost directly on down the field to a stile at the end of a footbridge. Over the footbridge our route goes up the field. keeping near to the hedge on the left. and then through a field gate and up the track to a lane at 6.

6.(117924) Our route turns right on the lane and then turns left at the T-junction to just past the first house on the right. Here our route turns right off the lane and over a stile on to a track between two hedges. At the end of the track our route goes over a stile and continues across the field to turn left, at 7. on the Coast Path which is fairly obvious back to Boscastle.

Boscastle and Rocky Valley.

Entering Boscastle on the B3263 from the north east there is a car park on the left near the visitor centre at 1.

10km (6 miles).
The scenery is very good. The in[...] combines woodland and open far[m...] good views.
Overall from 15m up to 212 metr[es] Some modest slopes.
There is a car park at 1.
There are tearooms at Rocky Valley, Trethevey and Boscastle and pubs in Boscastle.

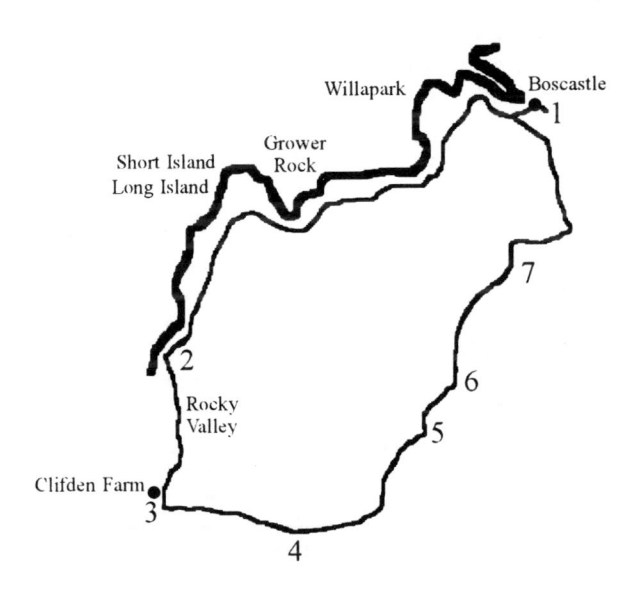

1.(098914) From the car park our route follows the main road down towards the old harbour for a few metres to join the Coast Path and then goes across the road bridge over the River Valency. The Coast Path turns to the right and off the main road when the road bends sharply to the left. From here on the Coast Path is fairly obvious to Rocky Valley where our route leaves the Coast Path at 2.

2.(072895) Rocky Valley is about 4km south of Boscastle and is where the Coast Path zigzags down and then goes across a stream on a footbridge. After the footbridge our route turns left up the right bank of the stream and continues up the valley to a road. Across the road our route follows a lane for about 400m to a cluster of cottages and the farm buildings at Clifden Farm at 3.

3.(072887) Just past the cottages a path leaves the lane to go over two stiles on the left and then goes across the field, keeping a little to the left, down to a small gate through which our route enters a wood. Through the wood our route crosses the river over three footbridges and then goes past a ruined building on the right to reach a cluster of buildings and a wooden bungalow called The Hermitage on the right at 4.

4.(081885) Here our route turns right, around the garden, and soon comes to a stile over which our route enters a field.

...n here on our route continues through ...ields and near the stream to a ruined house from where our route follows a marked path that continues up the valley, over the brook and on to a lane on which our route turns left to Tredole Farm at 5.
5.(091891) Here our route continues on the lane to where the road bends to the left and two footpaths go across the field on the right. Our route goes over the stile on the right to go diagonally up and across the field to a stone stile in the corner and then on to a lane. Here our route turns right for about 100m, past the entrance to Trehane Farm, and then left through a field gate and on to a track at 6.
6.(092895) Our route continues along this track to where it bends to the left and here our route turns off over a stile on the right and follows a footpath diagonally across the field, approximately towards the distant church that is between the houses and the cliffs, to a stile and a footbridge. Beyond these our route goes through the first gate on the right and continues across the field, approximately towards the church, and then down and around the side of the same field to go over a stone stile on the right into another field. Continuing across this field our route goes over a stile in the opposite hedge, about 20m up from a gate. Over this stile our route continues across the field and slightly downhill to another stile and on to a track at 7.
7.(095902) Turning left on this track our route goes down to a lane called Paradise Road and turns right on it. Continuing along Paradise Road to a crossroads our route turns left down a lane called High Street and then continues on down Fore Street to the bridge over the River Valency and then to the car park, at 1, on the right.

Parts of Boscastle harbour are described in Thomas Hardy's poetry and Beeny Cliff, which is near one of the walks in this booklet, was one of the places were he used to write.

The original inner harbour at Boscastle was built in the late 16th century and looking down into it from the cliffs it is difficult to believe that such a difficult harbour was once the main port for this area and Launceston, exporting slate and corn and importing food and coal.

Further down the coast are Port Isaac and Portquin. Port Isaac once had a good trade in pilchards and slate whereas Portquin was a hamlet of fishermen and miners at the Doyden antimony mines. The miners emigrated when the antimony mines failed and in a storm many of the remaining men were killed whilst fishing. Hence the ruined buildings by the path.

South of Portquin the coast shows increasing signs of the mining history of the county. Near New Polzeath the car park is at a very ancient mining site and south from St. Agnes ruined engine houses become numerous.

Tintagel, Trebarwith Strand and Rocky Valley.

The B3263 south from Boscastle goes through Tintagel. There are many places to park in Tintagel and there are also many access points on to the Coast Path from Tintagel. The most straightforward route is probably to follow the signs from Tintagel to the castle and then turn left on to the Coast Path at 1.

9km (6 miles).
The scenery is good. Most of the inland part is over almost level typical local farmland. Can be muddy in winter.
Overall from 20m up to 140 metres. Some modest slopes and a steep one.
There are car parks at Tintagel, Trethevey, Trebarwith Strand and at 6 which is on the B3263 near the top of Rocky Valley.
There are tearooms at Tintagel and Rocky Valley and pubs at Trebarwith Strand, Treknow and Tintagel.

1.(052890) From Tintagel the Coast Path is fairly obvious south to Trebarwith Strand. Trebarwith Strand is easily identified as the first place where a road comes down to the sea and is about 2.5km south of Tintagel. As the Coast Path starts to descend to Trebarwith Strand there is a path on the left at 2.
2.(050867) Here our route leaves the Coast Path and follows this path for about 250m up to join a track between two houses called The Bluff and Gull Rock. Our route continues to the end of this track and then turns right on the tarmac lane as far as a stone stile on the left that is opposite Atlantic Close at 3.
3.(056870) Our route goes over this stile and along a footpath by the side of a

garden to another stone stile from where our route goes directly across a small paddock, over a stile and into a field. Directly across this field our route goes through the field gate and continues across the next field keeping to the right of the hedge to the first stone stile on the left. Over this stile our route goes diagonally up and across to near the top corner where there is a stone stile on either side of the road and after going over these continues across two small fields and two stone stiles to a farm at 4.

4.(060873) The farm is Tregeath Farm and opposite where our route comes on to the lane in front of the farm there is a stile into the farmyard. Our route goes over the stile and across the farmyard to pass between the new buildings and the old buildings to leave the yard through a field gate. A few metres ahead and slightly to the left there is a field gate in a hedge. Through this gate our route turns right and continues with the hedge to the right, past a small gate in the hedge on the right, to cross three fields and to go over three stone stiles into a field with a hedge that is just slightly to the left and which continues ahead. Our route goes diagonally across this field to go over a stone stile in the corner and then continues approximately in the same direction across the next field to pass through the left gateway of the pair of field gates up in the far right corner in a hedge and then across the field to go over a stile in a hedge. From here our route goes across the field with the hedge to the right of our route and continues over a stone stile in a hedge and directly across the next field to a stile on the right, near the corner at 5.

5.(069879) Over the stile our route turns left along a track and on to a lane where our route turns right and, bearing to the left, joins another lane on which our route turns left for about 1km to a road at 6.

6.(072890) Almost directly across the road is a track down Rocky Valley to the Coast Path, at 7(072895), where our route turns left to return to Tintagel.

Beside the path through Rocky Valley there are some small rock carvings dating from between 1400 and 1800 BC.

No evidence has ever been found to support the legendary connection of Tintagel with King Arthur who led the locals to battle against those nice Saxon visitors 600 years ago but now all is peaceful and a whole industry has grown up for tourists around the mythology of this Celtic King. The high cliffs of Tintagel Head and the narrow spur that connects it to the mainland make an impressive setting for a castle.

St. Agnes has more of a recent history where mining continued into the early part of this century. Before steam engines were invented the miners burrowed into the cliffs and hills to seek out copper and tin and signs of these workings can still be seen.

Trebarwith Strand, Dannonchapel Valley and Treligga.

On the B3263 about 3km (2 miles) south of Tintagel turn right on to the minor road signed to Trebarwith Strand. There is a car park on this minor road.

11km (7 miles) or two walks of 6km (4 miles) and 5km (3 miles).
The scenery is very good.
Overall from almost sea level up to 181 metres.
Some modest slopes.
There is a car park at Trebarwith Strand.
There are tearooms at Tintagel and pubs at Trebarwith Strand and Treknow.

1.(058863) From Trebarwith Strand the Coast Path south continues just inland of the pub and is fairly obvious for the 3.5km to Dannonchapel Valley at 3.

3.(034829) Dannonchapel Valley is where the Coast Path comes down into a shallow combe and a footbridge crosses a small stream, where there is an area of exposed rock about 40m wide to the sea, where on the south side the Coast Path continues up and to the left around a cleft in the cliff, where at the right time of the year the south side of the valley is covered in cowslips and on the near side there is a large patch of thrift. Here our route leaves the Coast Path and turns left, before the footbridge, up the valley to follow a path along the left bank of the stream and to then follow the path up the side of the valley to a stile. Our route goes over this stile, into a field and turns right for about 10m to then go over another stile and continue directly on to the farm which is Tregragon Farm at 4.

4.(046831) Our route continues through the farm on the track which continues past the top of a conifer plantation and on to a lane where our route turns left. The lane continues to Treligga and from the telephone kiosk continues as a track at 6.

6.(051844) Our route continues along the track to bear left at some very old buildings on the right and just at the end of the buildings, before the track bears to the right, there is a field gate on the right. Our route goes through this gate and along the left side of the field to a stone stile by a field gate. Over the stile our route continues along the left side of the field, past a field gate on the left and on to a small gate in the hedge. Our route goes through this small gate into a field. Directly across this field there are two field gates and our route goes through the one on the left into a field. Directly across this field our route goes through a gateway, continues across another field to go through a field gate and on to a track which leads to the buildings of Trecarne Farm at 7.

7.(055854) At Trecarne Farm our route continues around the seaward side of the farm buildings to go through a field gate, then between the farmhouse and the farm buildings and then left around the inland side of the farmhouse to continue past some old buildings and down through some trees to a stone footbridge. From the footbridge our route continues across the field, near the hedge on the right, to go over a stile, past a house called Belsloe and on to a lane. Our route turns left on the lane for about 300m to where there is another lane on the right at 8.

8.(056860) A few metres further on our route goes through the field gate on the left. At the far end of the field a sunken track goes down between two hedges and our route follows this track along to where another track joins it on the left. Our route continues directly on and around the valley side to join the Coast Path just before the pub at Trebarwith Strand.

SHORT ROUTES.

Trebarwith Strand Part. 6km. This path follows the Coast Path south from Trebarwith Strand for about 2km to Tregardock Cliffs at 2(044842) which is where the Coast Path comes down through some bracken and low scrub and another path comes down the valley to cross the Coast Path about 200m inland. Here one path is signed to the beach, the Coast Path continues on upwards and our route leaves the Coast Path and turns left on a path that goes up through the valley for about 125m to a field gate. Our route goes through the small gate by the side of the field gate and then continues up the track to where it bears right between two hedges. Here our route leaves the track and turns left across the top of the field and then goes over a stone stile near the corner into another field. Our route goes across this field near to the hedge bank on the right, over another stile and then continues near to the hedge bank on the right to a field gate. Through the field gate our route goes along a short track to a lane on which it turns right to a T-junction near a telephone kiosk at Treligga. Our route turns left on the lane to 6 and then follows the main notes from where the lane becomes a track.

Dannonchapel Part. 5km. Parking at Tregardock is very restricted. On the B3314, just over 1km south of Delabole, there is a turning off to the right to Treligga. Tregardock is down the first turning on the left off this lane.

Towards the furthest end of this lane to Tregardock, just after the first farm building on the right, our route goes down a footpath on a track, through a small gate, and then keeps to the left, down through the valley, to a small gate. Through this gate our route continues down through the National Trust property called Tregardock Cliffs for about 125m to turn left at 2, on to the Coast Path, which is fairly obvious to Dannonchapel Valley, at 3, from where the main notes indicate the route to Tregragon Farm at 4. At Tregragon Farm our route continues through the farm on the track which continues past the top of a conifer plantation and up towards a lane. About 100m before the lane our route goes over a stone stile on the left, at 5(052834), and then immediately over a wooden stile to continue diagonally across the field towards a field gate in the hedge on the left and a few hundred metres from the furthest side of the field. Through this gate our route continues down the field and slightly to the right to a field gate on to the lane near Tregardock.

Portquin and Port Isaac.

From Wadebridge take the B3314 north for about 7km (4 miles) to a very sharp right bend. Continue directly on to a minor road signed New Polzeath for just over .5km to a staggered crossroads. Portquin is about 1.5km straight over the crossroads on a very minor lane. There is a car park at 1.

7km (4 miles).
The scenery is very good.
Good walking all year but only if sh[e]
are enjoyed. Most of the cliff path ha[s]
forced into an exceptionally narrow a[r]
between the cliff top and a very stout fence.
Overall from 10m up to 75 metres.
Some modest slopes.
There are car parks at Portquin but parking facilities at Port Isaac are very limited.
There are tearooms and pubs in Port Isaac.

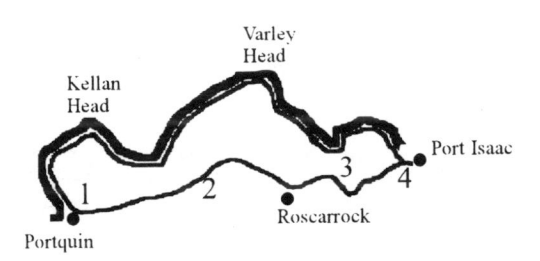

1.(969804) From Portquin our route continues on the minor lane past some small derelict cottages on the left that are overgrown to where the lane bends to the right and about twenty metres further on there is a field gate, past some cottages on the left. Our route leaves the lane and goes over the stile by the side of the field gate and continues up the valley for about .5km and then begins to progressively climb up towards the left and towards two field gates at 2.

2.(980806) Here our route goes over the stone stile and continues on a track that curves around to the right towards the left of Roscarrock Farm which can be seen over on the right. When the track goes into a field and bends sharp right to go across to the inland side of Roscarrock our route turns left to continue near the left side of the field and then right to a stile in the hedge at 3.

3.(988806) Our route goes over the stile and turns right to continue down to a footbridge. Over the footbridge and the stile our route goes directly up the hill, keeping to the left of the lookout post on the top, and continues to a stone stile in the bank on the Port Isaac side of the field. Over this stile our route goes almost directly down a track, over another stone stile, and then continues down the path to join the Coast Path on a tarmac drive at 4.

4.(994807) Port Isaac is a hundred metres or so to the right and to the left the Coast Path is fairly obvious back to Portquin.

Page 16

Pentireglaze, Pentire Point and New Polzeath.

5km (3 miles).
The scenery is very good.
Usually good walking all year round.
Overall from almost sea level up to 80 metres.
Some modest slopes.
There is a car park at 1.
There are tearooms and pubs in New Polzeath and a tearoom at Pentire which is past the car park at 1.

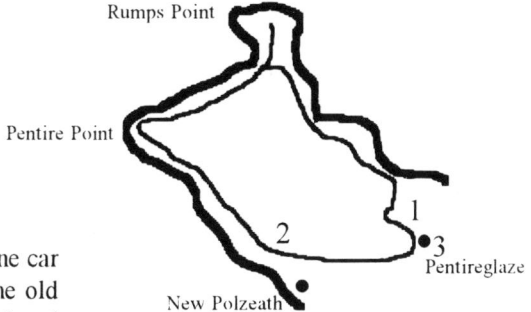

From Wadebridge take the B3314 north for about 7km (4 miles) to a very sharp right bend. Continue directly on to a minor road signed to New Polzeath for just over .5km to a staggered crossroads. Turn left at this crossroads and bear to the right at the next two forks to remain on the road signed to New Polzeath for about 2km and then turn right on a very minor lane signed to Pentireglaze. Continue through the farm to a car park on the right signed Old Lead Mines car park at 1.

1.(941800) From the Old Lead Mine car park our route goes up and over the old mine workings, across a small field and through a small gate on to the Coast Path. Our route turns left on the Coast Path which is fairly obvious all the way round to 2.

2.(936796) Just before New Polzeath the Coast Path comes down to a cove where a track also comes down to the beach. Here our route leaves the Coast Path and goes inland on the track, past the bungalow on the left called Penglaze, to a field gate. Through the field gate our route goes across four fields on the remains of an old track to a gate on to a lane at 3.

3.(944797) Here our route turns left on the lane to Pentireglaze Farm where it turns left to return to the car park at 1.

Page 17

Padstow, Stepper Point and Trevone.

12km (7 miles) or 8km (5 miles).
The scenery is very good.
Usually good walking all year.
Overall from sea level up to 70 metres.
Some very modest slopes.
There are car parks at Padstow, at Trevone and at 8.
There are tearooms and pubs in Padstow and Trevone.

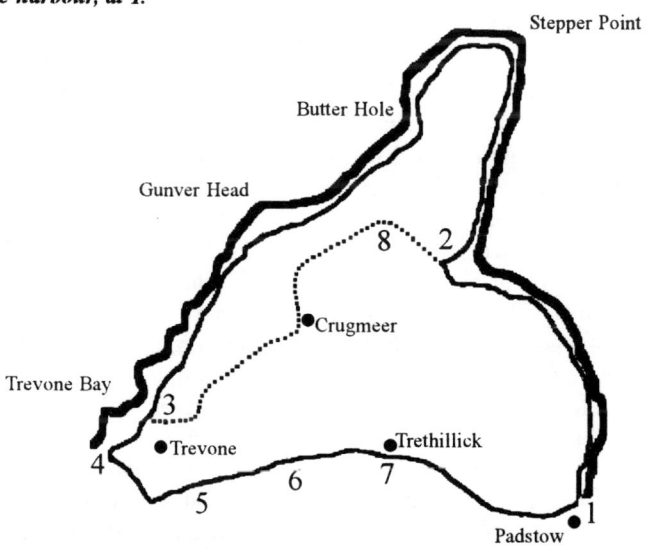

Padstow is on the north west end of the A389. In summer, parking in Padstow is extremely difficult and it is usually preferable to park in the large car park on the right hand side near the end of the A389, above the town, and then follow the signs down to the quay. This walk starts opposite the Tourist Information Centre near the north end of the harbour, at 1.

1.(919755) From almost opposite the Tourist Information Centre at Padstow Harbour our route follows North Quay Parade up to Chapel Style Field and then continues on the path along the right edge of the field. From here on the Coast Path is signed and is fairly obvious around Stepper Point and to 3, at Trevone Bay, where the Coast Path comes down a few steps and joins a lane on which it turns right down to a small bay.

3.(892760) The Coast Path goes around the bay, between the sea and the buildings, and then, after the buildings, continues between a field bank and a small cliff to 4.

4.(887758) Here the Coast Path goes past a few seats and bears left through a small gate into a field and in the field our route leaves the Coast Path. Through this gate the Coast Path turns right along the cliff side of the field but our route continues up the left side of the field on a footpath that is close to the field bank. At the top of the field our route turns left through a gateway and across the top of the adjacent field for about 25m. Then our route goes over the stile by the side of the gate on the right and continues up the right side of the field to the top where it turns left on the path near the hedge bank to another stile next to a gate. Over this stile our route goes across the top of the field and on to a track to continue past the pub on the left and then turns left on a road for a few metres. Our route then takes the first turning on the left on to a lane to the post office which is on the left at 5.

5.(893755) At the post office in Trevone our route joins a road on a bend and continues directly along the road to the next bend where our route turns off to the right, on to a lane. When the lane bears left to become a track there is a small gate into the field directly ahead. Our route goes through this gate and across the field, keeping slightly to the left, to a stile. From this stile a small farm can be seen almost directly ahead. Our route goes towards this farm to go over a stile near the bottom of the field. In the next field our route keeps close to the hedge on the left to cross the small brook on a large slab of stone and to then go over a stile and into a field. Our route goes across the field and through a gateway into a farmyard at 6.

6.(899757) Our route goes diagonally up and across the yard, through a gateway and on to a track that continues past the house on the right and directly on to a stone stile. Over this stile our route continues almost directly across the next field to a stile that can be seen in the opposite hedge. Over that stile our route goes across the next field, keeping slightly to the left, to go over the stile in the opposite hedge and then continues across the field to a field gate. Over the stile next to the field gate our route turns right on a lane and continues to a crossroads at Trethillick, at 7.

7.(906756) Here our route turns right on the road and then turns left over a stile on the near side and at the far end of the first stone barn on the left. Over this stile our route goes across the field towards the gate in the corner. Just before the gate our route goes over the stone stile on the left and then continues across the field, almost in the same direction, to go over a stone stile and on to a lane. Our route turns right on the lane to the T-junction where the left turning goes down in to Padstow and the right turning goes up to the A389. The car park above Padstow is just along the A389 on the left.

SHORT ROUTE. 8km. From where the A389 ends at Padstow continue on the B3276 for just over .5km to a crossroads and turn right on a narrow lane for about 2km through Crugmeer and to a car park on the right, at 8(906772), just before Lellizzick.

Our route follows a permissive path down and across the car park to a stile in the furthest corner and goes over the stile and continues down a track. When the track bears sharp left, on the edge of the trees, our route turns left on to the Coast Path, at 2(910770), and up the steps. The Coast Path is fairly obvious to 3 at Trevone Bay which is where it comes down a few steps to join a tarmac lane. Here our route leaves the Coast Path and turns left up the tarmac lane for about 1km to a T-junction at Crugmeer. At the T-junction our route turns left on a lane which returns to the car park, at 8.

St. Agnes Head, Porthtowan and St. Agnes Beacon.

From the B3277 in St. Agnes follow the minor road northwest from the bend almost opposite the church. Continue for just over 3km (2 miles) to the National Trust car park at 1 which is on the corner of a junction on the right, where there is heath over St. Agnes Beacon on the left. There are more parking areas on the lane to St. Agnes Head.

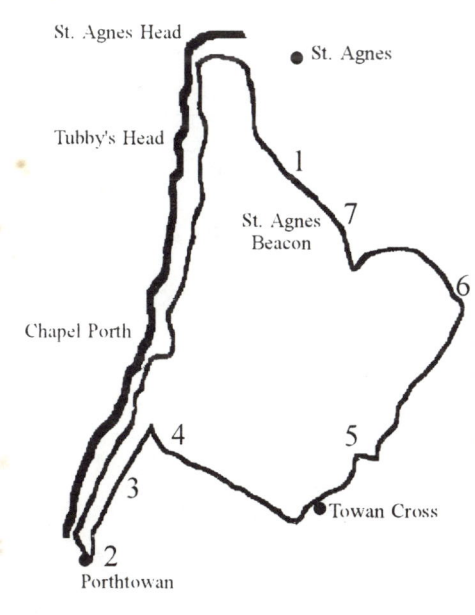

10km (6 miles).
The scenery is good. T[...]
good and the inland se[...]
farmland with good vi[...]
Beacon.
Usually good walkin[...]
From 10 metres up to 19[...]
Some modest slopes.
There are car parks at 1 and at Porthtowan.
There are tearooms and pubs in St Agnes and Porthtowan and there is a pub at Towan Cross.

1.(706506) From the National Trust car park our route continues down the adjacent lane towards the sea and turns off right to follow the path down the left side of the lookout to join the Coast Path at St. Agnes Head. Here our route turns left on the Coast Path which is fairly obvious for about 3.5km to Porthtowan which is the first large village south at 2.

2.(693481) The Coast Path comes down to a car park at Porthtowan from where our route follows a footpath that is above the Coast Path to a seat near the corner of the garden of a bungalow above. Here our route continues for about 50m and then follows the first vague path up on the right and eventually arrives at a small gate at 3.

3.(695486) Our route goes through the small gate and continues near a bank on the right. When this bank bends right our route continues on across the fields and then goes through another small gate on to a track on the heath. Here our route goes across the heath to a join the first track on which it turns right to where another track joins from the right at 4.

4.(700488) Our route continues on the same track to where it curves to the right and then leaves the track to continue straight on along a path that goes through the gorse to the road nearly opposite the pub. Our route turns left on the road and then turns left down the lane opposite the Victory Inn to cross the brook and turn right at the next lane on the right at 5.

5.(711488) About 125m along this lane there is a track on the left, just before a field gate. Our route turns left along this track to just before a field gate where it continues as a path through the scrub to much smaller path, that is quite missed, goes off on the right. Our route follows this path on the right towards the fields on the right and then continues alongside the field bank to reach a stile on the right into the field. Our route goes over the stile and turns left in the field and continues along the left side of numerous fields and stone stiles to the first stone stile on the left which is just before a bank that is almost under some overhead power lines. Here our route turns left to go over the stone stile and to continue along the right hand side of the field to go over another stile on to a track that leads on to a lane on the outskirts of St. Agnes at 6.

6.(716500) Our route goes across the lane and up a track to go across another lane and continue up a farm drive that ends near the farm buildings at Beacon Farm. From here our route continues up a track into, and across, a field to a stone stile. Our route goes over the stone stile and on to a path across the heath for a few metres to then go up the hill on a small path on the right. Our route goes up the path to pass in front of a seat in front of the rock and then on to the triangulation point on top of St. Agnes Beacon at 7.

7.(711503) From the top of St. Agnes Beacon two paths lead off along the ridge towards the sea. Our route follows the left path down to the car park at 1.

UPDATES.

To avoid reprinting all of the text the alterations to routes that have taken place subsequent to printing are shown here.

Portreath, Coombe and Tehidy Country Park.

Entering Portreath on the B3300, from the A30 near Redruth, there is a car park on the right at 1, near the shore just before the B3300 bends to the left to go over a bridge. There are two more car parks on the Coast Path and just off the B3301 at about 2km and 3.5km (2 miles) south of Portreath.

10km (6 miles). This walk is easily combined with the walk to Hell's Mouth.
The scenery is very good. Most of the inland part is through mixed woodland.
Usually good walking all year round.
From sea level up to 80 metres.
Some modest slopes.
There are car parks at 1, 2 and 3.
There are tearooms and pubs in Portreath.

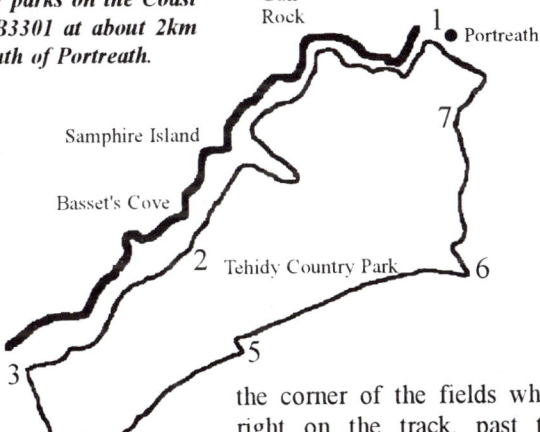

1.(654453) From the car park at Portreath our route goes on to the main road and turns right over the bridge and then right again up Battery Road to where there is a pair of garages and a sign to the left of them indicating the North Coast Footpath. The Coast Path is fairly obvious for about 4km to a National Trust car park on the cliff top at 3.

3.(626431) Here our route leaves the Coast Path to go along the track, directly across the road and over a stile, down the left side of the fields and on to the lane where it turns left for about 200m to a track that shares the entrance with the house on the left at 4.

4.(630425) Our route follows this track, past the house on the right, into and through the wood for about 1.5km to a junction very near some fields at 5.

5.(642433) Here our route turns left to the corner of the fields where it turns right on the track, past the disused hospital on the right, and continues past the golf course on the right to a road at 6.

6.(659439) Here our route turns left on the road for about 200m to turn right on the track at the end of the wood. Our route goes along this track to a farm where it turns left at the junction with a concrete farm road and then takes the first concrete farm road on the right down into the farmyard at 7.

7.(659448) As the road enters the yard our route leaves the road to follow a footpath near the fence that goes down into the wood on the left. Our route follows the footpath down and to the right and then follows another path off to the left which continues down through the valley to a lane where our route turns left. At the next lane our route turns left, and at the bottom of the hill goes under an arch, bears right over a bridge and then left to return to the car park at 1.

Hell's Mouth and Coombe.

Travelling south from Portreath for about 3km (2 miles) on the B3301 there is a track on the right to a National Trust cliff top car park at 1. The track is directly opposite a stile into the fields on the left.

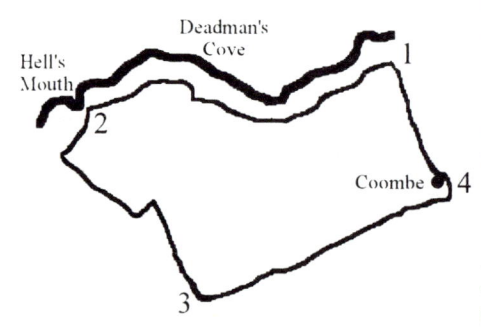

7km (5 miles). This walk could be combined with the walk from Portreath.
The scenery is very good. The inland part is over farmland and through wetland shrubs and trees.
Very wet and muddy in winter.
Overall from 28m up to 80 metres.
Some modest slopes.
There is a car park at 1.
There is a tearoom at Hell's Mouth and there are pubs at Portreath.

1.(626431) From the car park our route follows the Coast Path west for about 2km to Hell's Mouth which is where the Coast Path comes to within 20m of the road, where there is a 200ft cliff and there is a cafe just across the road at 2.

2.(603429) Here our route leaves the Coast Path to follow the footpath down the side of the cafe to a path that runs along the near side of the wood that is along the bottom of the field on the right. Just before a ruined cottage in the wood our route turns left and goes down through the wood on a footpath with a small bank to the right of it. Then our route goes across a brook and through a small gate to continue up the left side of the field to a field gate on to a lane. On the lane our route turns left to a stile into a field on the right that is opposite the entrance to Carlean Farm. Over this stile our route goes along the left side of the field and over another stile near the corner in the opposite hedge. Over this stile our route continues down the left side of the field to go through a field gate in the lower left corner into the field on the left at 3.

3.(611417) From this gate our route goes across the field and slightly downhill to a gate in the opposite hedge through which our path continues along a track to just before the farmhouse on the left where it follows the track down to a lane. Our route continues directly along the lane until it bends up and to the left to go past some buildings. At this bend our route leaves the lane to go down a track on the right to where it bends left into a property called Goonzoyle. At this bend our route goes through the gate on the right and continues in the same direction but on another track to a tarmac lane at 4.

4.(629423) Here our route turns left on the lane and then left again over a bridge on to another lane and continues up this lane for about 200m to a footpath that goes through a small gate just past a house on the right. Our route follows this path up the right side of the field to go through a small gate and continues up the right side of the next field to go over a stile and on to the road opposite the car park at 1.

Page 23

St. Ives, River Cove, Wicca and Trevalgan.

10km (6 miles) from St. Ives, 8km (5 miles) from Wicca.
The scenery is outstanding. Not only is the coastal scenery outstanding but the inland area between the coast and the moorland is very scenic.
Usually good walking all year round.
Overall from sea level up to 130 metres.
Some modest slopes.
There are tearooms and pubs in St. Ives.

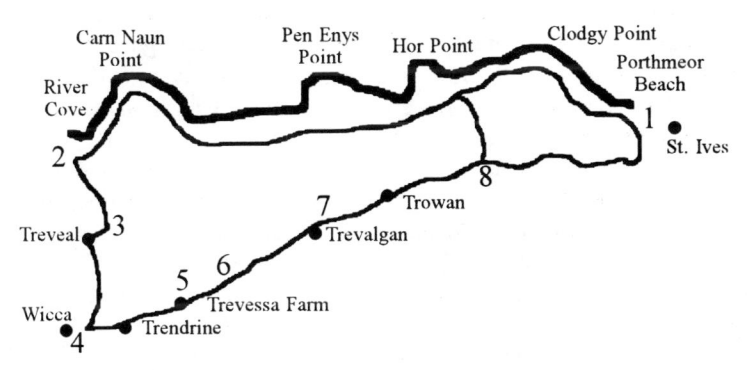

From the A3074 into St. Ives there are signs to the car park for Porthmeor Beach at 1. From the car park the Coast Path can be seen going north west to Clodgy Point. Alternatively, on the B3306 heading south west and about 3km (2 miles) from the outskirts of St. Ives there is an easily missed track on the right with a small sign to Wicca where parking is possible, near 4. The track forks soon after leaving the road and Wicca is at the end of the left fork.

1. (515408) From Porthmeor Beach in St. Ives the Coast Path is fairly obvious for just over 4km to River Cove which is where the Coast Path comes down into a bracken covered valley with some rock outcrops between the path and the sea and then the path goes across a brook. As the Coast Path goes up the other side of the valley there are some rocks out to sea and a path leads inland up the right side of the valley from 2.
2. (473405) Here our route leaves the Coast Path to follow this inland path up the right side of the valley to where it joins a track at 3.
3. (474401) Here our route turns right and then continues around the house at Treveal, on the left, and on up the track. Near the top of the slope the track bears right to pass some farm buildings on the right and at this bend our route leaves the track to turn off left to go over a stile at 4.
4. (473394) From this stile our route goes across the top of the field to go over another stile and across the top of another field to reach a stile by a field gate next to the buildings at Trendrine. Over this stile our route keeps to the left of the building that is directly ahead and then goes over another stone stile from where it continues towards the right hand

Page 24

side of the farm that can be seen across the valley. On the way our route goes over the stile in the opposite hedge, then continues directly across the corner of the field to go over another stone stile on the left, down across the field towards the farm, over a stone stile, across another field and over another stone stile, across a small paddock keeping slightly to the left to go over another stone stile and over a stone footbridge and then up the next field to go through two small gates at the right hand end of the barn and on to a lane at Trevessa Farm at 5.

5.(481397) Our route turns left on the lane for a few metres and then follows the first footpath on the right between two buildings, through a gate and over two stone stiles into a field. Our route goes across the field and over a stone stile in the far left corner into another field. Our route goes across this field and over the stone stile in the far right corner and then directly across another field to go over another stone stile and on to a lane at 6.

6.(485399) Our route turns right on the lane and then takes the next footpath on the left that goes down a short track, over a stone stile by the side of the field gate and into a field for about 15m to then go over a stone stile on the left and to continue across the field, with a bank on the right, and then through a gap in the corner and into the next field. Across this field our route goes over another stile and across the next field towards the left side of the cluster of buildings where our route goes over a stone stile, across the field with the buildings of Trevalgan on the right, to another stone stile at 7.

7.(490404) Over this stile our route goes across the right hand side of the field, over another stone stile, across another field, over another stone stile, across the next field keeping slightly to the left and towards the next farm, over another stone stile, across the left side of the next field, through a field gate, across the left side of the next field, over another stile, into the next field for a few metres to go over the stile on the left and on to a path between the houses and in to a farmyard at Trowan. Through the farmyard our route goes directly on to a lane where it turns left for a few metres and then right over a stone stile into a field, across the left side of the field to go over another stone stile, directly across the next field to go over another stone stile, across the next field keeping slightly to the left to go over another stone stile by a field gate, across the field to go over another stone stile, directly across the next field to go through a gap in the bank, across the next field to a stone stile, across the right hand side of the next field to go through a gap, across the next field to go over another stile, directly across the next field to go over the stone stile by the side of the field gate and on to a track at 8.

8.(502406) If this walk was started at Wicca and if it is preferred not to go into St. Ives then the Coast Path can easily be reached by turning left down the track. To get to St. Ives our route goes across the track, over the stone stile and continues across rough grass and bracken, across small fields and three stone stiles and into a field on the far side of which the field extends down to the left where our route continues on a track. Our route leaves the track by going over the first stone stile on the right and into a field where it turns immediately left to go over the stone stile down in the corner and then down a path between two hedges to go over another stone stile on to a track where it turns right to St. Ives.

Page 25

Zennor, Wicca, Zennor Head and Poniou.

From St. Ives follow the B3306 south for about 5km (3 miles) to Zennor which is well signed and where parking is usually available at 1, which is between the pub and the museum. Parking is also available at Wicca Farm which is on the right about 3km (2 miles) south from St. Ives on the B3306. The sign to the farm is very small and the track to the farm forks soon after leaving the road. Wicca is at the end of the left fork.

10km (6 miles).
The scenery is outstanding. Not only is the coastal scenery outstanding but the inland part through ancient fields between the coast and the moorland is also very scenic.
Usually good walking all year round.
Overall from 30 metres up to 130 metres.
Some modest slopes.
There are car parks at Zennor and Wicca.
There are tearooms and pubs in St. Ives and a pub in Zennor.

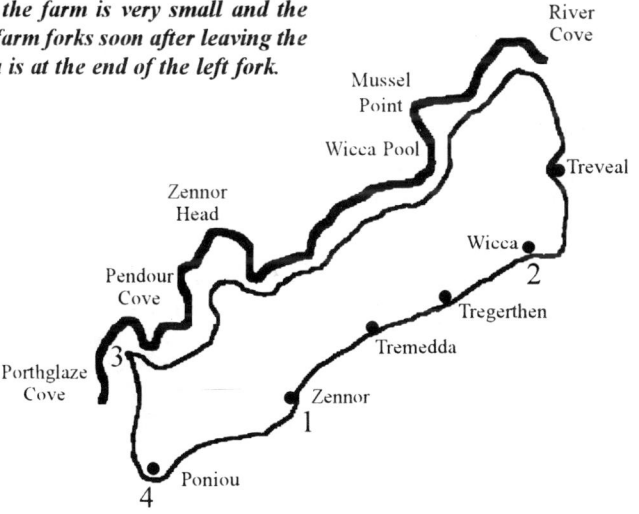

1.(454384) From the car park near the museum in Zennor our route continues on the lane towards the church where it curves to the left and then follows the footpath on the right around the west end of the church to go over a stile. From here to Wicca, which is about 2km, the footpath heads northeast and goes through only one gateway and this is a few fields before Wicca. Between all other fields this route only ever goes over stone stiles, the first few of which are marked with white paint. After these the farm buildings at Tremedda can be seen and the route passes close to the right of these. After Tremedda the farm buildings at Tregerthen can be seen and the route passes close to the right of these. After Tregerthen the route eventually goes past a ruined house or barn and then continues through the scrub, then over a stile and then almost directly across the field to go through a gap/gateway. From this gap the route continues across the field and only goes over stiles from here to the farmyard at Wicca at 2.

2.(471395) From the farmyard at Wicca our route continues along the farm track for about 150m and then bears left at the fork on a track that goes down to Treveal. At Treveal it curves around the farm house which is on the right and then continues down the track to the first footpath on the left signed to River Cove. Our route follows this footpath down the left side of the valley to turn left on the Coast Path which is fairly obvious to Porthglaze Cove just before which our route leaves the Coast Path at 3.

3.(443388) This point can be recognised where the Coast Path comes around a head and there are some bare rocks above and also between the Coast Path and the sea. where there is usually a waterfall at the apex of the facing cove and where there is a bungalow up on the top of the cliffs all of which is about 1km after the first cluster of buildings that can be seen from the Coast Path after River Cove. Here our route leaves the Coast Path to follow a small path that goes up the slope and then goes behind the bungalow to join a track that goes inland for about 750m to a cluster of houses at Poniou at 4.

4.(444380) Our route turns left on a track that runs in front of the houses and when this track bends left our route leaves the track and continues over a stone stile on the right. From here to Zennor the route is approximately north-easterly and only goes over stone stiles. never through gateways. on the way. At Zennor our route follows the footpath down a track. with a farm on the right. on to a road. Our route turns left on the road and then immediately left down a minor road to Zennor at 1.

This walk was one of the last to be done for the South West Coast Path series and it was walked in winter on one of those days when the sky was clear blue with some patches of modest cumulus clouds perched up on the moor.

The drive to it is through an extremely pleasant area. Looking down on to those small and ancient fields and then out to sea provides a picture in itself but to walk through it and around it can provide a variety of shades and colours not always available on the Cornish coast.

But the area not only offers colours. It offers an aura of timelessness seldom found on mainland Britain. Above Zennor, up on the moor, is Zennor Quoit, a tomb from the early Neolithic period that was covered with a mound about 37m across and made by the people who preceeded the permanent farmers.

The stone walls were built more than a thousand years later by the Iron Age people and although the Romans no doubt came and went they left no obvious trace of occupation but Wicca is one of the few Saxon names in the area from a thousand years ago.

And still the fields and the scene remain relatively unchanged; except by the seasons.

Woon Gumpus Common, Pendeen Watch and Bosullow Common.

From Newlyn follow the A3071 west for about 7km (4 miles) and turn right on to the B3318 for about 2km (1.5 miles). About 200m before the B3318 forks there are areas on the right that are used for parking at 1.

Between Trehyllys Farm and the bridge in paragraph 3 our path follows tracks, lanes and paths that are frequently used by the public but which are not necessarily public rights of way.
13km (8 miles) or 10km (6 miles).
The scenery is very good. Not only is the coast scenery very good but the inland part includes moorland and farmland.
Usually good walking all year round but can be muddy in places.
Overall from about sea level up to 225 metres. Some modest slopes.
Parking is possible at 1 and there is a car park near the lighthouse at Pendeen Watch.
There are tearooms and pubs in St. Just.
There is a pub in Pendeen.

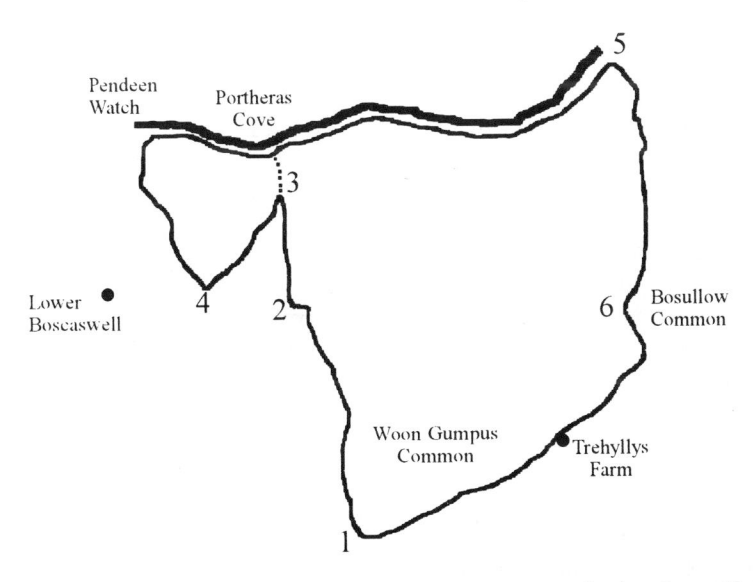

1.(395331) Where the fields end and the moorland begins an obvious track comes across the edge of the moorland from the northeast to the road. About 20m in from the road a track turns off to the left, towards the coast and continues near to the road. Our route follows this track towards the coast for about 150m and then joins another track to continue towards the coast. This track continues to go slightly away from the road to a junction of tracks. Here our route turns right on a track that immediately forks and our route takes the left fork. This track goes very slightly down to go through an area that can be wet and then up to a fork. Our route takes the left fork to go through some low gorse to where the top of an almost triangular field comes up to this track from the left. Ignoring the track on the left before the field our route turns left on the track immediately after the field and follows this track down over the moor, and then between the fields to the road at Higher Bojewyan. Our route turns left on the road for about 200m and then turns right on to the first lane at 2.

2.(390348) Our route follows this lane and when the lane bends sharp right towards the farm our route continues on down a track to a stile by the field gate. Over this stile our route goes down the grass track for nearly 500m to enter a small triangular field. Here our route follows the grass track as it curves to the left to go down through some gorse to a bridge at 3.

3.(390355) Over the bridge our route continues up the opposite slope, keeping to the right of the old stone wall, to go over the stile by the side of a gate and to continue on a narrow track between two stone banks into the farmyard at Portheras Farm. Our route turns left on to the lane that runs out of the farmyard and after the farmhouse on the right our route goes over the first stile into the first field on the right. Our route continues to the far left corner of the field where it goes over the stile and continues along the right side of the next field for a few metres to go over the first stile on the right into another field. From here our route continues along the right side of the fields, past the farm and cottages at Calartha Farm on the right, to go over two last stiles on to a farm track. Here our route turns left towards the road at 4.

4.(384349) Our route turns right on the road down to the lighthouse at Pendeen Watch where our route joins, and turns right on the Coast Path which is fairly obvious for about 3.5km. About 3km after our route has joined the Coast Path, the Coast Path comes noticeably close to the road where, on the opposite side of the road, the bracken comes down quite a steep slope to the road. Progressively the Coast Path moves away from the road and there are some fields between the Coast Path and the road before the next footpath which leaves the Coast Path to go inland at 5.

5.(414364) Here our route goes inland to the road where it turns right for just a few metres to then go up through the bracken on the first bridleway, which is signed. The bridleway winds up through the bracken to arrive near the top on the left of some redundant mine buildings. From here our route continues, south, on a very obvious track to join a lane at 6.

6.(415347) Our route turns left on the lane for about 300m to turn right on to the first lane. This lane continues for just over 1km to Trehyllys Farm where it curves around to the right and just past the last house on the right curves to the left and continues as a track near the edge of the moor for about 1.5km back to 1.

SHORTER ROUTE.

Over the bridge at 3, instead of going up the slope, turn right and slightly uphill to join a path that goes down the left side of the valley to join, and turn right on, the Coast Path above Portheras Cove.

Sennen Cove and Maen Dower.

About 3km (2 miles) before Land's End on the A30 turn right on to the minor road signed to Sennen Cove. At the bottom of the hill there is a car park near the beach, on the right, at 1.

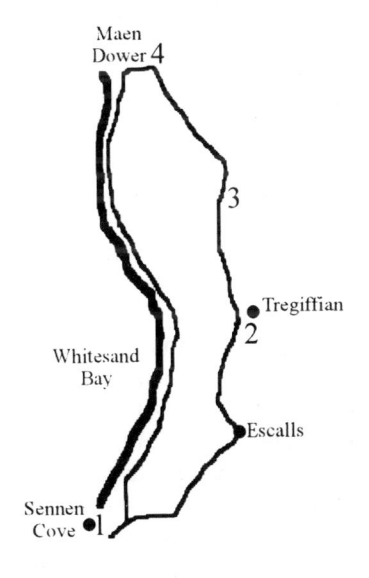

The inland part of this walk includes tracks, lanes and paths that are frequently used by the public but which are not necessarily public rights of way.
8km (5 miles).
The scenery is good.
Usually good walking all year round.
Only very slight slopes.
Overall from sea level up to 100 metres.
There is a car park at 1.
There are tearooms and a pub at Sennen Cove.

1.(355263) From the car park the Coast Path north is signed as it continues near to a wooden fence and on to pass between the two cottages at the left end of a row. Here our route leaves the Coast Path to follow a track on the right to go up to a field gate where our route turns right on a lane for about 25m. Here our route turns left, off the lane, to go up a track signed as a footpath and to then go over a stile and into a field. Our route continues across the field, over another stile, across another field and over a stile about 10m to the left of a field gate and on to a track near Escalls. Turning right on the track to just past the turning on the left our route then turns left, off the track, to pass to the left of the house called Wellfield, and then directly across the field to go over a stile and on to a lane. On the lane our route turns right to the first junction and then turns left along a lane, keeping to the tarmac, and keeping to the right when the lane forks, for about three quarters of a kilometre to 2.

2.(367278) This is where the lane has gone around a sharp right bend, then a sharp left bend and then bends sharp right again. Here our route goes through the field gate, across the field on the track to the other side and turns right down the side of the field or headland to the first stone stile on the left. Over this stile our route continues across the field to go over another stile and then directly across another field to go on to a lane by a field gate at 3.

3.(365286) Our route turns right on the lane to a junction and then turns left on another lane that becomes a track and continues for about 900m from the junction to a path that turns off to the left near the far side of the converted mill at 4.

4.(360294) Our route continues along the path near the side of the mill to join the Coast Path near Maen Dower and turns left back to Sennen Cove.

Sennen Cove, Land's End and Mill Bay.

8km (5 miles).
The scenery is very good.
Usually good walking all year round.
Overall from about sea level up to 101 metres.
Some modest slopes and a steep one.
There is a car park at 1.
There are tearooms and a pub at Sennen Cove.

On the A30 turn right about 3km (2 miles) before Land's End on to a minor road to Sennen Cove. At Sennen Cove continue to the car park at 1 which is at the end of the road, near the lifeboat station.

1.(349263) From the car park our route follows the Coast Path south for about 3km to go through the Land's End complex and the adjacent small animal farm to 2. at the far side of Mill Bay.

2.(357238) At the far side of Mill Bay a house can be seen on the other side of a valley through which a small brook flows. Our route leaves the Coast Path to follow the signed footpath that follows a fairly well worn path up the near side of the valley and along the top of the near side of the valley, to go through a gate and into a field. Our route goes directly across the field to a pair of gates in the corner where it goes over the stile by the left gate and around the right side of the field to continue through a gateway and diagonally across the next field to the furthest corner. Here our route goes over the stile next to the gate and on to a track that goes around the right hand side of Trevilley and at the first T-junction goes straight across into a farmyard at 3.

3.(358245) Our route goes straight across the farmyard, over some concrete steps, around the right hand side of a field, over a stone stile and across the left side of a field to go through a small gate, over another stone stile and in front of the cottages to the road at 4.

4.(356248) Our route turns left on the road and then goes straight across at the T-junction to go down the drive to Treeve Moor House. As the drive bears left our route leaves the drive to continue on and then right to go over some stones, or an ancient stone stile, and into a field. Our route goes directly up the field to go through a small gate near the top left corner and into another field. Continuing across the top of this field our route then goes over a stone stile in the corner and on towards the houses to go over another stile on the coast side of them. Our route goes across the top of the field until the wall on the right ends and here our route goes through a small gate on to a lane at 5.

5.(352259) Our route continues in the same direction along the lane to follow it around to the right and on for about a further 300m to take the footpath down on the left which is before the last bungalow. At the end of the footpath our route turns left on the road to return to the car park at 1.

Porthcurno, Penberth Cove, Nanjizal and Gwennap Head.

From Newlyn take the B3315 towards Land's End for about 11km (7 miles) to a minor road on the left signed to Porthcurno. There is a large car park on the left at 1.

11km (7 miles) or two walks of 8km (5 miles) and 6km (4 miles).
The scenery is very good.
Usually good walking all year but can be muddy in places.
Overall from about sea level up to 93 metres.
Some modest slopes.
There is a large car park at Porthcurno.
There is a tearoom and a pub at Porthcurno.
There is a pub at Treen.

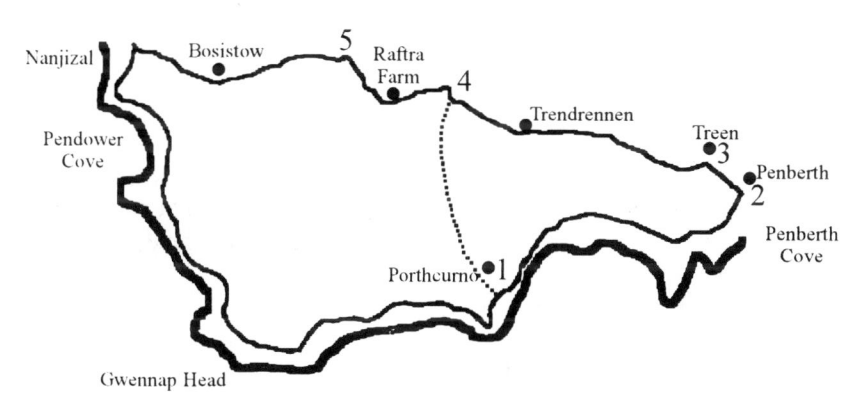

1.(385225) Before the minor road bears round to the right and starts to go uphill our route turns off to the left to join the Coast Path which is fairly obvious to Penberth Cove at 2. 2.(403227) Penberth Cove is fairly easy to recognise. Much of it is owned by the National Trust, it is an active small fishing cove and there is a large capstan near the Coast Path. Our route turns left before the capstan and before the brook to follow a footpath up the valley to go through a field gate on the right hand side of a cottage. (From here to Treen our route follows frequently used paths which are not necessarily public rights of way). Our route follows this footpath as it begins to climb the hillside and when the path starts to go down our route turns off to the left on a path that winds its way up the hill. This path curves to the left and then curves to the right on its way up through the wood to a field. In the field our route turns right to go around the field and before the gateway goes through the small gap and over a bank into a field. Our route continues across the field close to the bank on the left. When the field widens our route goes just to the left of straight on, and then, unless signed otherwise, goes over the bank where there appears to be the remains of a stone stile or through the gateway and across the next field to just before the standing stone. Here our route turns left to go over a stone stile in the bank and into another field. Our route turns right into a field used as a car park at Treen, at 3.

3.(394230) Our route continues diagonally across this field to the car park entrance and on to a tarmac lane that goes past the chapel on the left. When the lane

bends right our route turns off to the left and keeps to the right at the next two forks to go through a gap, along the left side of a house and over a stile by the side of a field gate into a field. Our route goes around the left side of the field to continue on a fairly obvious path that goes over 6 stiles and through intervening fields to reach a track on which our route turns left down to a field gate at Trendrennen. Through this field gate our route turns right, to continue directly up the field to go through a field gate and into the lower right corner of a field. Our route goes diagonally to the left and up the field to go over a stile, across the right side of another field and on to a lane at 4.
4.(382233) Our route turns right on the lane for about 100m and then turns off to the left to go over the first stone stile on to a footpath. This footpath goes across the field to go over a stone stile and continues almost directly across another field to go over another stone stile, to the left of a pair of gates, in the corner. Over this stile our route continues across the field, keeping slightly to the right, to go through a field gate in the far right corner and then right over the stile next to the gate immediately on the right at Raftra Farm. Our route goes around the left side of the field, past some farm buildings, and, unless they have now marked some other way through to the main track on the left, turns left on a track near the bottom of the gardens, through a field gate, and then right along another track to join the wider track that goes up between the farms to a lane at 5.
5.(374235) Our route turns left on the lane for about 40m and then turns right on to another track for about 800m to pass between the buildings of Bossistow Farm and to continue to where the track forks.

Our route takes the left fork for about 100m and then turns off to the right along another track. When this track forks our route follows the track to the left, towards the bay, where our route turns left on the Coast Path which is fairly obvious back to Porthcurno.

SHORT ROUTES.

Penberth Cove Part. 5km. Our route follows the notes through to 4 where it turns left on the lane down to Porthcurno.

Nanjizal Part. 8km. From the car park at 1 our route goes back up the lane for about 1km to 4 from where the notes can be followed. 4 is fairly easy to recognise. The stone stile is near a dip in the lane and is before a short track with a few dwellings on the same side of the lane. From the stile Raftra Farm is directly across the fields.

Lamorna Cove, Boskenna, St. Loy's Cove and Rosemodress Cliff.

From Newlyn take the B3315 towards Land's End for about 5km to a minor road on the left signed to Lamorna Cove. There is a car park near the end of the road at Lamorna Cove at 1.

9km (6 miles)
The scenery is very good.
Overall from sea level up to 112 metres.
Some modest slopes.
There is a car park at 1.
There is a tearoom at Lamorna Cove and a pub at Lamorna.

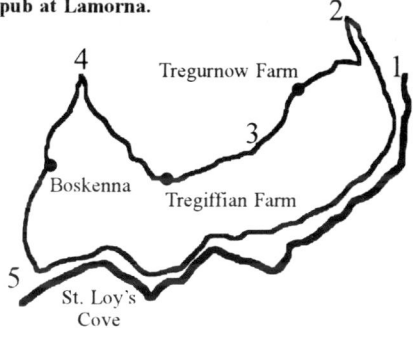

1.(450241) Our route returns up the lane to just past the Lamorna Wink at 2.
2.(446245) Our route follows the lane on the left for about 350m, turns off to the right on a track to a few houses and then follows the track as it curves to the left to Tregurnow Farm where it curves to the right and then follows a footpath off to the left immediately after the garden. After about 100m, our route goes over a stile on the left and then diagonally to the right to go over the stile in the corner, up the right side of the field to the next farm, Rosemodress Farm, and continues in approximately the same direction to join a track that is a little to the right at 3.
3.(441238) Our route follows this track between the buildings, across a lane, through a field gate and along the right side of some fields for about 600m to the next farm which is Tregiffian Farm. Here our route goes over the stile near the left side of the house and turns right on the lane for about 200m to follow the next signed footpath over the stile next to a field gate on the left. From here our route goes up the left side of the field, over a stile and then right on the track to the first group of buildings at Boscawen Rose. Here the rights of way appear to be through the farmyard on the left that is just before the first house on the right. Through this farmyard our route goes over a stile on the right by the end of the buildings and then diagonally to the left for about 50m to a corner, then along the right side of the field to the far end to turn left across the field and over a stile. From here our route goes across the field, over another stone stile, across another field keeping slightly to the right, over another stone stile and on to the far left corner of a field to a stile just before a road at 4.
4.(426242) Our route goes over the stile on the left and then turns left to the field gate near the right side of the bungalow at the far end of the field. On the way down there is a stile in the fence on the right. Through the gate our route continues directly on down the track to go through Boskenna and on for about 500m along the main track down towards the coast to where the main track bends sharp left and here our route leaves the track to continue directly on through a gate and down a track for a few metres. When this track bends sharp left our route continues directly on to go into the wood and then turns left on to a path that goes down the left side of the brook, over a bridge and then down to turn left on the Coast Path at a stile on the left at 5.(422231)

Perranuthnoe and Cudden Point.

5km (3 miles).
The scenery is good. The inland part is over typical farmland.
Good walking all year round.
Some modest slopes.
Overall from about sea level to 74m.
There is a car park at 1.
There is a pub in Perranuthnoe.

On the A394 from Penzance to Helston turn right about 8km (5 miles) from Penzance on to a minor road signed Perranuthnoe. Near the far end of the lane there is a car park on the left at 1.

1.(540294) From the car park our route goes down the lane and turns left on the track that runs along the lower side of the car park and then turns off on the first track on the right to follow the Coast Path for about 2km to Bessy's Cove where there are some houses and a letterbox in the wall on the left. A few metres further on the track forks at 2.

2.(557280) Our route leaves the Coast Path here and takes the left fork up to a lane where our route turns right. for about 500m. to a stone stile on the left and immediately past a field gate at 3.

3.(553285) Our route goes over the stile and across the field to go over another stone stile that is just to the right of the houses at the far end. Our route goes over this stile and directly across the field to turn right along the lower side of the field. over a stile. along the lower side of another field. over a bank and then part of the way along the lower side of the next field to go over a stile on the left and on to a rough lane. Our route turns right on the rough lane to the cluster of buildings where a good tarmac lane begins and then turns left down the farm drive towards Trevean Farm on a permissive path. When the farm drive curves left down to the farmhouse our route continues directly on for a few metres and then turns off to the right to go through a gateway. From this gateway our route continues to the top of the field where it goes over a stile and into a field. Our route follows a footpath along the right side of the field to go over a stile and across a yard to a tarmac lane at 4.

4.(545293) Our route turns left on the lane. which immediately becomes a track. and follows this track back to the car park.

Mullion Cove, Predannack Head and Ogo-dour Cove.

On the A3083, Helston to The Lizard, the B3296 turns off right at Penhale to continue through Mullion towards Mullion Cove for about 1km to a car park on the left at 1.

5km (3 miles).
The scenery is good.
Good walking all year round.
Some modest slopes.
Overall from about sea level up to 83m.
There is a car park at 1.
There is a tearoom in Mullion Cove, a pub on the road above Mullion Cove and a pub and a tearoom in Mullion.

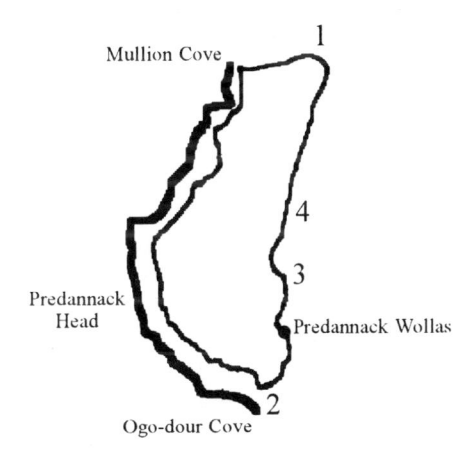

1.(672180) From the car park our route goes down the road to Mullion Cove. Just before the harbour the Coast Path is signed to the left and our route follows the Coast Path for about 2km to Ogo-dour Cove at 2. This is where the Coast Path comes down through some patchy scrub into a valley with a field on the left at the top of which can be seen the stone and white buildings at Predannack Wollas.

2.(669159) Just where this field ends our route leaves the Coast Path and goes inland on a path that is through the scrub but near the edge of the field. The path goes over a stile and then down to join a track on which our route turns left to continue between the farms and through the car park where it turns right on to a lane. Our route remains on this lane for about 250m to a stone stile on the left at 3.

3.(670165) Here our route goes over the stone stile on the left, across the field, over another stile and then slightly left of directly across the next field to go over a stone stile and on to a track on which our route turns right. When the track bears left our route leaves the track and continues straight on over a stile into a field and then goes around the left side of the field to a stone stile just before a field gate. Over this stone stile our route turns right up the lane to where it bends right.

Here our route leaves the lane and keeps straight on up the footpath that runs by the side of the house, over a stile into a field, up the right side of the field, over another stile and past an old stone cross on the right at 4.

4.(671171) Our route continues virtually in the same direction for almost 1km to go across the right side of the field and over a stile in the far right corner, across the next field and over a stile on the right about 50m before the corner, on to a path through the gorse and shrubs, over some stiles and small footbridges to a field. Our route goes across the right side of the field and over the stile in the far corner and on to a track. Our route turns left down the track to the road on which it turns right to return to the car park at 1.

Predannack Wollas, Vellan Head and Kynance Cove.

8km (5 miles).
The scenery is very good. Most of the inland part is through a nature reserve.
Muddy in winter.
Some modest slopes.
Overall from about sea level up to 80m.
There is a car park at 1.
There is a tearoom and a pub in Mullion.

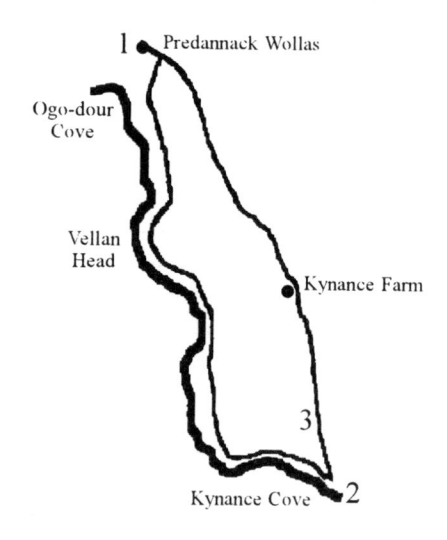

From the A3083, Helston to The Lizard, the B3296 turns off right at Penhale to continue through Mullion towards Mullion Cove. About 1km from the centre of Mullion a narrow lane, signed to Predannack, turns off to the left. There is a car park at 1, at Predannack Wollas at the end of the lane.

1.(669 162) From the car park at Predannack Wollas our route goes down the track between the farms to where the fields on the right end. Here our route turns right and continues over the hill to join the Coast Path on which it turns left, to just before Kynance Cove at 2.

2.(683 133) When it is possible to see the buildings down in the cove our route turns back to go along the small ridge, between both the valley that is now on the right and the coast, to a pair of gateways. Our route goes through the left gateway and follows a hardcore track to a field gate across the track at 3.

3.(682 138) Our route continues through the gate and along the track, to pass to the right of the houses at Kynance Farm. When the track bends left to go towards the houses our route keeps straight on along a less used grass track to go through the left of the two field gates and almost directly on. At the next junction with a stone track our route turns right and then turns off left through the first small gate into a field. Our route goes across the field and through a gap in the bank into another field where our route turns right and stays in this field to the far corner where it continues on across a field of heath and to a gate on the far side. Through this gate our route continues on a grass track to go over stiles and to reach a stile next to a field gate in a corner. Over this stile our route continues directly on along a track and remains on this when it bends to the left. Our route turns right when this track joins a slightly broader track on which it returns to the car park.

Page 37

The Lizard, Kynance Cove and Lizard Point.

The A3083 ends at the village of Lizard and there is a large parking area on the right, at 1.

6km (4 miles).
The scenery is outstanding.
Good walking all year round.
Some modest slopes.
Overall from sea level up to 74m.
There are car parks at 1 and just past 2.
There is a tearoom and a pub in The Lizard.

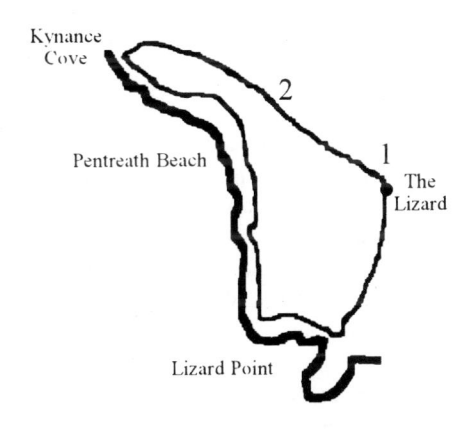

1.(703125) From the parking area an unnamed road goes due west along the lower side of the car park and continues past a bungalow on the right called Croft Pascoe. Just before the bungalow our route turns right off the road to go up some steps and on to a bank between the bungalow and a field gate. Our route goes along the top of the field bank to the end and then goes down some steps, through a small area of shrubs, then over a stone bank, across a field of low scrub, over another stone bank and across a field on a fairly obvious path to the stone stile in the furthest hedge at 2.

2.(695131) From the stile our route continues on to the lane for about 20m past the bungalow on the left called Carne Goon. Here our route follows the track that continues straight on as the lane bears left. Our route continues along the lane until it is near the corner of the National Trust Kynance Cove car park on the left. Here our route goes into the car park and about halfway across the bottom of it to a pathway on the right that goes down to Kynance Cove. Just before the cove our route turns off to the left to join the Coast Path for about 3km, around Lizard Point and on to a tarmac lane on which our route turns left to go up to The Lizard and the car park at 1.

The Lizard, Bass Point and Gwavas.

The A3083 ends at the village of Lizard and there is a large parking area on the right, at 1.

7km (4 miles).
The scenery is good.
Good walking all year round.
Some modest slopes.
Overall from sea level up to 75m.
There is a car park at 1.
There are tearooms and a pub in The Lizard.

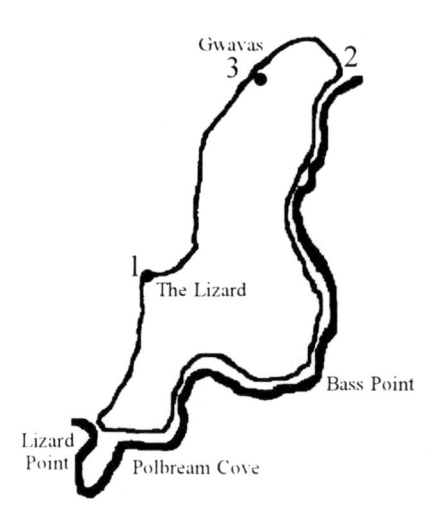

1.(703125) From the parking area a road goes down the side of the Top House Inn and from the Post Office this continues as Penmenner Road towards the sea. At the end of the road our route continues as a track and then as a path down to the Coast Path on which our path turns left for about 4km to 2. near Gwavas.

2.(718138) The Coast Path comes down through some scrub and goes over a stone bank where there is the corner of a field on the left. Immediately after the bank the Coast Path goes over a small brook and then immediately bears right to continue through the bushes but our route leaves the Coast Path immediately after the small brook to go over the stile on the left on a route that goes up through the bushes. At the top of this footpath our route turns left on a track that leads on to a lane. On the lane our route turns left and just past Gwavas Farm on the left, when the lane bends right, our route keeps on along a short track. At the end of this short track our route goes over the stile next to the gate and continues across the field to some steps up a bank at 3.

3.(712138) Our route continues along the top of the bank to the other end where it goes down the steps on the left and continues in approximately the same direction on a track for a few metres to where three tracks meet at Trethvas Farm. Our route keeps to the left to go down the track on the left and almost immediately over the stone stile by the first field gate on the right and continues across the right hand side of the field to go over a stile in the far corner. Our route then goes across the right side of a field, over a stone stile in the corner and continues in the same direction across a field, now with a hedge bank on the left to go over a stile and on to a road. Our route continues along the road in the same direction and the road then bears around to the right to return to the car park.

Porthallow, Nare Point and Gillan.

6km (4 miles).
The scenery is good.
Can be muddy in winter between Halwyn and Porthallow.
Some modest slopes.
Overall from sea level up to 80m.
There is a car park at 1.
There is a tearoom and a pub in Porthallow.

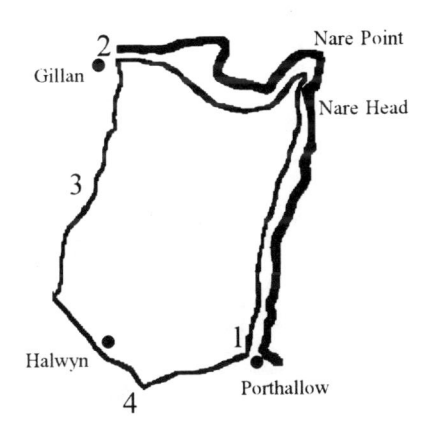

On the A3083 from Helston to The Lizard turn off left about 4km (3 miles) from Helston on to the B3293 to St. Keverne. From the centre of St. Keverne follow the narrow lane signed to Porthallow. There is a car park on the beach at Porthallow at 1.

1.(797232) From the car park at Porthallow our route follows the Coast Path north from the steps near the beach, around the top of the small cliffs and on for about 3km to Gillan which is the next village on the Coast Path. Our route leaves the Coast Path where the National Trust property called "The Herra" ends at Gillan Harbour which is the small bay with a stoney beach. Here a track comes down to the nearside of the bay just before a wooden shed at 2.

2.(787251) Our route goes up this track to turn right on another track at a field gate. Our route follows this track through the farm and up to a crossroads where four lanes/tracks meet at 3.

3.(786241) Our route goes directly across on to the tarmac lane and continues to the second lane on the left where our path turns left. A few metres before the far end of this lane there is a stone stile on the left at 4, just before the T-junction.

4.(788230) (In winter when there is a lot less traffic and a lot of mud most walkers would probably find it preferable to turn left at the T-junction and follow the lane down to Porthallow.) Our route goes over the stone stile on the left and diagonally across the field towards the left to come to a stone stile where a hedge once was. From here our route bears right to go down the right side of the field and over a stile in the furthest corner, across a track, directly over another stile and across the field in the same direction to leave the field through what was a small gate. Through the gate our route continues down through the bracken and near the bottom of the valley curves to the right, goes over a stile, through a small gate, along a track in front of a row of cottages and on to a lane. Here our route turns left to the car park.

Manaccan, Dennis Head and Helford.

On the A3083 from Helston to Lizard turn off left about 4km (3 miles) from Helston on to the B3293 towards St. Keverne. There is a car park very near the Coast Path just before Helford and Helford is signed off the B3293. There is a car park on the Coast Path at St. Anthony-in Meneage which is signed from Manaccan and parking is usually possible near 1, in Manaccan which is signed from the lane to Helford.

10km (6 miles).
The scenery is good.
Can be muddy in winter.
Some modest slopes.
Overall from sea level up to 60m.
There are car parks at Manaccan, Helford and St. Anthony in Meneage.
There is a tearoom in Helford. There are pubs in Manaccan and Helford.

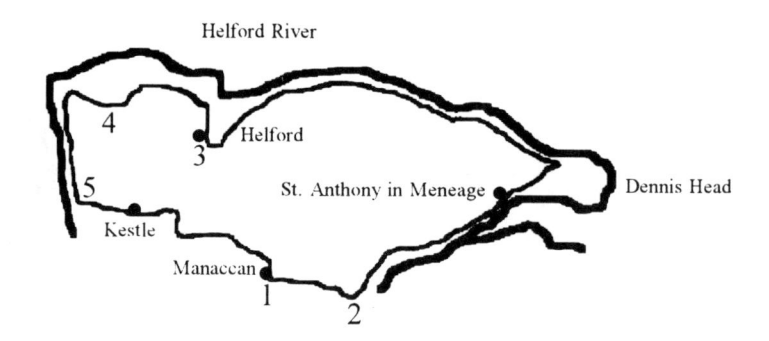

1.(764250) At Manaccan there is a road around the church and from this, just up from the post office, a lane turns off to the right, away from the church. Our route follows this lane for about 80m and then turns off right, down a narrow lane, for about 30m to go over a stile on the left and to continue around the right side of the field to go over another stile to the far right corner of the next field. Here our route goes over a stile to follow a path that goes down through the wood to cross the brook on a footbridge and then continues on to a lane. Our route turns left on the lane to the first junction at 2.

2.(770249) Here our route turns left on the lane that is around the left side of the estuary to St. Anthony in Meneage where our path joins the Coast Path. As the lane bends up and around the church the Coast Path turns off to the right on a permissive path to Helford at 3. The Coast Path is fairly obvious to Helford although there are a couple of places where it joins lanes where the route is not waymarked. At both of these the Coast Path goes down the hill.

3.(758259) In Helford our route follows

the Coast Path across the river and continues around the waters edge to just past the pub where our route leaves the Coast Path to go up the lane on the left for about 100m to then turn right on a footpath to Penarvon Cove. Here our route goes across the beach and then follows a footpath that runs atop the small cliff and then up some steps on the left to some buildings. At the buildings our route turns right and follows the track up and to the left to join a lane on which our route turns right up to a bend at 4.

4.(753260) Here the lane continues to the left but our route goes down the farm track on the right almost to the bottom of the field and then turns off left on a footpath that goes down some steps and through some scrub to continue through the wood for just under 1km to join a concrete track at 5.

5.(749256) Our route turns left up this track and at the top of the track continues on a path around the right side of the farm on to a lane. Our route goes directly across the lane to go through the yard of Kestle Farm. At the far end of the farmyard our route heads towards two gates and goes through the right hand one into a field and continues down the left side of the field to a stile. Over the stile our route goes down through the wood, across a brook, and then turns right on a track which bears around and up to the left to arrive at a stile. Over this stile our route goes across the field to where the trees jut out into the field and here our route bears slightly to the right to cross the remainder of the field and go over a stile onto a lane. Almost directly across the lane our route continues along the left side of the field to a lane in Manaccan where the church is a few metres to the right.

The walk around Cudden Point offers some good views back along the coast to St. Michael's Mount.

Lizard Point is the most southerly point in Britain.

Gillan Harbour may be very quiet now but it was a very busy medieval port before it silted up.

At Dodman Point the earthworks are the remains of an Iron Age Fort.

At Gribbin Head the red and white striped beacon was erected in the middle of the 19th century as a day beacon for shipping.

Polruan may now be a sleepy village but in 1066 it was probably the main port on the Fowey Estuary.

Everywhere else there is the sound of the waves, the breeze and the bird song; the colours, shades and hues of everything the way it naturally is; the infinite variation of shape and form within the natural world.

Percuil River, Zone Point and Porthmellin Head.

On the A3078 from Tregony to St. Mawes turn off left at Trewithian on to the minor road to St. Anthony. Just over 4km (3 miles) from Trewithian, just past Froe where the road is close to the estuary, there are two National Trust car parks on the right at Porth Farm at 1.

9km (6 miles).
The scenery is good.
Good walking all year round.
Some modest slopes.
Overall from sea level up to 40m.
There is a car park at 1.
There is a tearoom and a pub in Gerran about 2km from this walk.

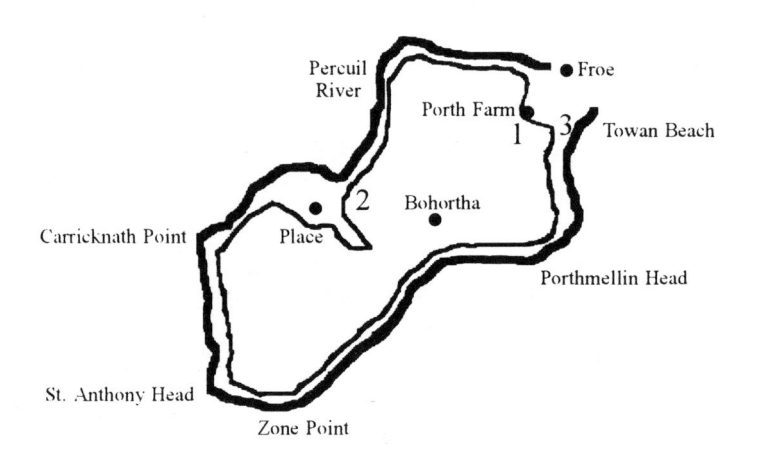

1.(867329) From the lower of the two car parks our route follows a path down, near the lane, to a footbridge signed to Place. Over the footbridge our route turns right to follow the path around the field edge, over a stile in the corner and into the wood. Through the wood our route ignores both of the paths off to the left and after about 2km arrives at a stile. Over this stile our route goes across the right side of the field to go over another stile on to a lane near a slipway at 2.

2.(855323) Our route turns left on the lane and follows the Coast Path for about 5km to Towan Beach at 3. The Coast Path goes up the lane, past the entrance to Place House and is then signed to the right from where on it is fairly obvious to Towan Beach.

3.(870326) Towan Beach is where the Coast Path comes down through some bracken to the corner of a field and then continues across the bottom of a small field where the roofs of some buildings at Porth Farm can be seen over to the left and a beach begins on the right. Our route turns left on the path that runs inland from the beach and, just before the lane, turns left to follow the path through the buildings to come out on to the lane opposite the car park.

Penare, Hemmick Beach, Dodman Point and Gorran Haven.

8km (5 miles).
The scenery is good.
Good walking all year round.
There are some modest slopes.
Overall from 10m up to 112m.
There is a car park at 1.
There is a tearoom and a pub in Gorran Haven.

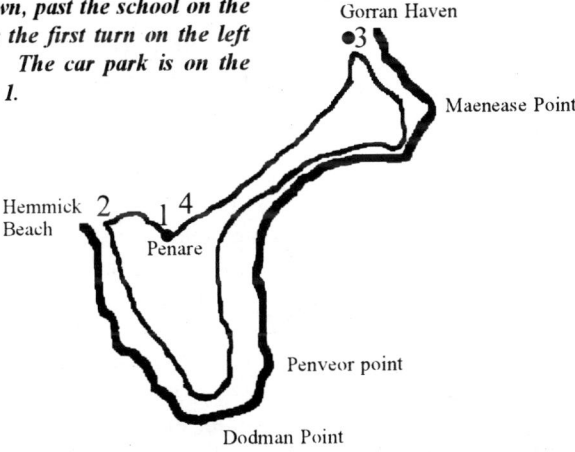

On the B3273, St. Austell to Mevagissey, turn off right about 6km (4 miles) from St. Austell on to a minor road signed to Gorran Haven. Take the first turning right in Gorran Churchtown, past the school on the left and then take the first turn on the left signed to Penare. The car park is on the right in Penare at 1.

1.(999404) From the entrance to the car park in Penare our route goes across the lane and turns right on the footpath. Our route follows this footpath over a stile and then down the edge of the field near the side of the lane to just before Hemmick Beach where it turns left on the Coast Path at 2. In the winter when there is little traffic and the field is muddy it can be preferable to go down the lane to 2.
2.(995405) From here the Coast Path is signed and is fairly obvious to Gorran Haven at 3.
3.(013416) Gorran Haven is the only coastal village on this walk and here our route follows the Coast Path down some steps to turn left on the first lane which is Foxhole Lane. Our route goes up this lane to the T-junction where it turns left on another lane that continues as an unfenced lane to 4.
4.(002405) Where the unfenced lane leaves the field at a field gate there is a stone stile on the left. Our route goes over this stile and diagonally down across the field to another stone stile which is about half way along the hedge bank. Over this stone stile our route goes to the left and around the field to go over the next stile and left on to a lane. On the lane our route continues directly to the car park.

Fowey, Polkerris and Gribbin Head.

About 2km before Fowey on the A3082 from St. Austell the B3269 joins at a roundabout. Continuing towards Fowey on the A3082 turn right on to the first minor lane signed as unsuitable for large vehicles. There is a car park at the end of this lane at 1, at Coombe.

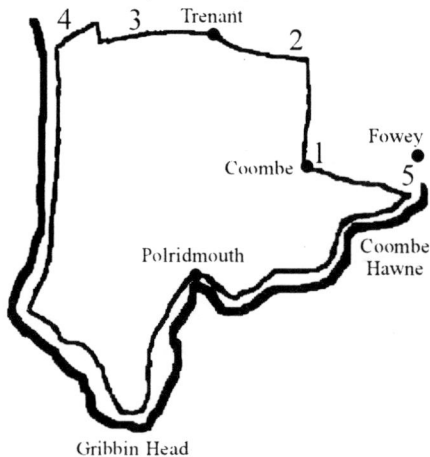

10km (6 miles).
The scenery is very good.
Can be muddy in winter.
There are a few modest slopes.
Overall from about sea level to 74 m.
There is a car park at 1.
There are tearooms in Fowey. There are pubs in Fowey and Polkerris.

1.(110512) From the car park our route goes back up the lane for about 600m to just past Lankelly Farm House on the left, at the junction. Here our route follows the footpath on the left that continues down through the second gate on the left and then between the oak trees at 2.

2.(110518) Our route continues down the track, across the brook, under the bridge and then up the track with the old stone walls. At the top our route leaves the track and goes directly over a stone wall and continues across the right side of the field to Trenant. Here our route follows a track between the farmhouse on the right and the ruined buildings on the left to a stile. Over the stile our route follows the footpath directly across the left side of the field, across a footbridge and through a gate into a field where our route continues around the left side of the field to a stile by a disused stone building at 3.

3.(099520) Our route goes over the stile and into the field to cross the bridge and continue up the field to a field gate near the right hand corner of the farm buildings at Tregaminion. Through this gate our route goes up a track to a lane where our route turns right for about 100m to the first field gate on the left. Our route goes through this gate and follows a footpath across the field to the wood on the other side where our route joins the Coast Path at 4.

4.(095520) Here our route turns left and follows the Coast Path for about 5km to a wood on the outskirts of Fowey at 5. The Coast Path is fairly obvious but it is possible to mistake an inland path at Polridmouth for the Coast Path.

5.(118509) Just before this point the Coast Path goes up from Coombe Hawne and then across the edge of a field and in to the wood at 5. Within a few metres our route turns left through the wood on the good path nearest the top of the wood that goes inland to a gate at the top far corner. Through this gate our route continues on approximately the same contour across the field, over a stile next to a field gate and along the track to the car park at 1.

Pencarrow, Pont Pill and Polruan.

Before entering Polperro on the A387 turn off right on to a minor road signed to Bodinnick or to Fowey via ferry and then turn off to the left towards Polruan. The area is a maze of very small lanes. The car park at 1 is at Pencarrow and adjacent to the lane that runs nearest the coast from Triggabrowne to Polruan. After Triggabrowne take the first lane on the right and the entrance is on the right.

7km (4 miles).
The scenery is good.
Good walking all year round.
There are some modest slopes.
Overall from sea level up to 112 m.
There is a car park at 1.
There is a tearoom and a pub in Polruan.

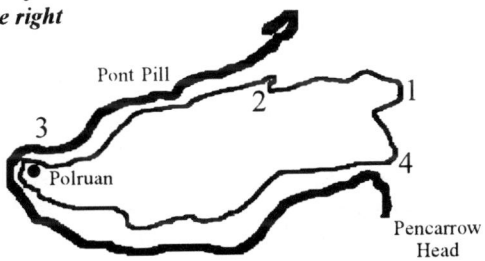

1.(150513) From the entrance to the National Trust car park at Pencarrow our route turns right down the lane and past the church on the right to continue along a gated lane to a T-junction just past a small picnic area on the right at 2.

2.(140514) Our route turns right at the T-junction to go down the lane for about 100m to a field gate on the left. Our route goes through this gate to immediately turn left on a path and then immediately right at the fork to go downhill on a path through the wood. When the path forks again our route goes to the left to a tarmac lane on which our route turns right for a few metres to then turn off to the left to continue on the path. At the end of the path, at the bottom of the concrete steps at Polruan, our route turns right down some more steps and at the bottom of these turns left along a narrow street which leads to a small square with the quay down on the right at 3.

3.(125510) Our route goes directly across the small square to go up West Street, past the Methodist Church on the left, and then up Battery Lane on the left. Our route continues up Battery Lane, past the tarmac lane on the left, to bear round to the left. When the tarmac ends our route continues on the Coast Path which is fairly obvious and signed either with acorns or as a footpath to Lantic Cove. About 3km from the quay at Polruan, after the Coast Path has gone along the side of two cliff top fields and has then gone gradually down through some bracken, it arrives at a stile at the corner of a field at 4.

4.(149510) Many walkers find the view from Pencarrow Head over on the right to be worth the walk but our route turns left immediately after the stile to go through the field gate into the adjacent field. Our route continues up the right side of the field to go over a stile on to the lane where it turns right back to the car park.

Cawsand, Rame Head and Penlee Point.

This walk starts in Cawsand. Turn right, when travelling towards Torpoint, off the A374 at Antony on to the B3247 to Millbrook and then right again between Millbrook and Cremyll on to the minor road to Cawsand.

8km (5 miles).
The scenery is very good.
Good walking all year.
A few modest slopes and a steep one.
Overall from 20m up to 110m.
There is a car park at Cawsand and at 3 on the coast road.
There are tearooms and pubs at Cawsand and Kingsand.

1.(432502) Near St. Andrews Place in Cawsand there is a car park at 1 and from the car park our route continues inland on a minor road and turns right on to a lane called Hat Lane. Near the top of the hill our route turns left down a farm drive to Wringford Down and Wringford Farm and, before the farmhouse, turns right on a footpath between two hedges and continues into a field at 2.

2.(425505) Our route continues across the field, bearing gradually to the left, to go through a gate and then down a path with hedges to both sides. Our route keeps to the left side of the farmhouse at the farm called Wiggle and joins a lane. Here our route turns left on the lane for about 500m to a car park between the lane and a road at a junction. Our route turns right to cross the road just before the car park at 3.

3.(419503) From here our route goes down the slope on the other side of the road to join the Coast Path which is fairly obvious all the way back to Cawsand where it comes down Pier Lane. Then our route turns off, inland and up St. Andrews Place to the car park.

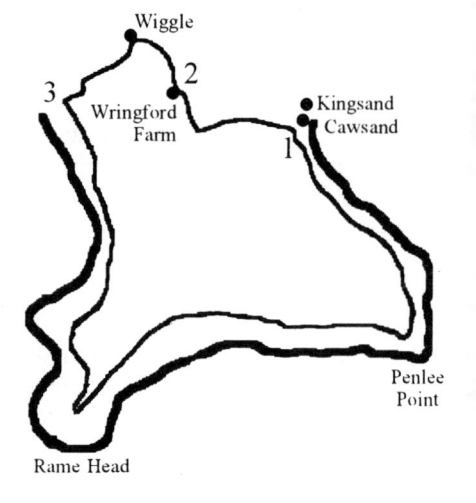

Page 47